ALSO BY CLAIRE BIDWELL SMITH

The Rules of Inheritance

After This: When Life is Over, Where Do We Go?

Anxiety: The Missing Stage of Grief

Conscious Grieving

ANXIOUS GRIEF

ANXIOUS GRIEF

A Clinician's Guide to

Supporting Grieving Clients

Experiencing

Anxiety, Panic, and Fear

CLAIRE BIDWELL SMITH, LCPC

ANXIOUS GRIEF
Copyright © 2023 by Claire Bidwell Smith

Published by
PESI Publishing, Inc.
3839 White Ave
Eau Claire, WI 54703

Cover and interior design by Emily Dyer
Editing by Molly Gage, PhD

ISBN 9781683736974 (print)
ISBN 9781683736981 (ePUB)
ISBN 9781683736998 (ePDF)

PESI Publishing
pesipublishing.com

CONTENTS

Preface v

Introduction ix

CHAPTER 1: Serving as a Companion to Grief 1

CHAPTER 2: Listening to the Story of Loss 13

CHAPTER 3: Understanding Grief 23

CHAPTER 4: Normalizing the Grieving Process 35

CHAPTER 5: Responding to Grief Anxiety 49

CHAPTER 6: Approaching Family, Work, and Lifestyle Dynamics ... 61

CHAPTER 7: Utilizing Mindfulness and Meditation 73

CHAPTER 8: Strategies for Grief 87

CHAPTER 9: Strategies for Anxiety 117

CHAPTER 10: Strategies for Anger 153

CHAPTER 11: Strategies for Guilt 173

CHAPTER 12: Cultivating Self-Compassion and Resilience 197

CHAPTER 13: Exploring Religion, Spirituality, and Ritual 221

CHAPTER 14: Finding Connection and Purpose 247

About the Author 259

PREFACE

We bereaved are not alone. We belong to the largest company
in all the world—the company of those who have known suffering.

—Helen Keller

In May 2020, I worked almost every single day inside my house, alongside my husband, while my three kids spent their school days at the kitchen table on Zoom. Since the pandemic had begun, the demand on me as a grief therapist had tripled. I found myself frantically trying to rise to the occasion while grappling with the many changes in my own life resulting from the new realities of living with COVID-19.

Not only was my decade-long career in the field of grief and loss asking me to meet demand like never before, but the paperback version of my newest book, *Anxiety: The Missing Stage of Grief,* had just been released. When I wrote that book, I never could have imagined that it would arrive on shelves during a time when the entire world was experiencing grief and anxiety.

The truth is, grief and anxiety are a regular occurrence in our lives. I'm sorry that it took the emergence of COVID-19 for the population at large to understand this, but I can find gratitude that since 2020, we have begun to recognize how important it is to understand and cope with these two very difficult, but very human, experiences.

Grief and anxiety have played large roles in my life, beginning with my mother's death when I was a teenager and continuing into my forties in my work as a therapist. I didn't grow up wanting to be a grief therapist. I wanted to be a writer. As the only child of much older parents, I had a solitary childhood, and books were my best friends. I read copiously, disappearing for long hours into stories and worlds that weren't mine. By the time I had reached adolescence, I was writing my own stories. I was drawn to books about the human experience, stories about adversity and overcoming hardship. Perhaps this was a result of having parents who had lived such varied and layered lives. Perhaps it was the result of the near-simultaneous cancer diagnoses they received when I was still a girl.

My adolescence was upended by my parents' diagnoses. While my friends enjoyed more typical teenage experiences of life, I sat in hospital waiting rooms, helped my mother through chemotherapy treatments, and watched my father struggle to grapple with the mounting medical bills. No one ever talked to me about what I might be feeling or experiencing. Instead, I was encouraged to go about life with as much normalcy as possible. I tried to bury myself further into my books, but among the surging troubles of my own life, these stories were no longer enough of a distraction, the fictitious worlds not deep enough to escape within. Nothing felt normal. In fact, trying to uphold my idea of normal landed me in the emergency room at 18 years old—my first panic attack—shortly before my mother died.

In the ER, the doctors checked me out head to toe, studied my bloodwork, ran a series of diagnostic tests, and declared me fit and healthy. They never asked me about my personal or emotional life. I hadn't known to tell them. If they *had* asked, I would have told them that both of my parents were sick with cancer and that I was about to leave home to follow my dream of becoming a writer at a college thousands of miles away from them. Instead, I left the ER thinking there must be something else wrong with me. I couldn't stay calm. I didn't feel healthy. But most of all, I felt an overwhelming inability to simply . . . be normal. No one in my life could help me connect my anxiety to the threat of my parents' looming deaths, so in turn, I chalked it up to personal failure.

Six months after my visit to the hospital, my mother died while I was away at college, and the floor dropped out from beneath me. My family and I had been so afraid to talk about what would happen if she died that we just didn't talk about it at all. In turn, I was completely unprepared, and because I was unprepared, I wasn't with my mother when she died. It took me years to acknowledge and understand my grief and its manifestations in my anxiety.

My father's cancer had been less severe than my mother's, and he lived for seven years after her death. During those years, I inhabited a dark world of grief and anxiety without a clue as to where to turn. The support people in my life once again told me that I would be fine and urged me to stay on track—keep the "normalcy" of life going. But there was nothing normal happening inside. I silently battled my panic attacks and phobias, stayed shrouded in grief, and plunged headlong into school, pursuing a career in writing.

When I was twenty-five years old, my father's cancer returned once again—for what we would learn would be the last time. My mother had sought treatment after treatment, trying experimental medicine and interventions, until she finally died, never facing the reality that the end of her life was near. But when my father received his last diagnosis, he chose instead to embrace his death. He enlisted the services of hospice, and I cared for him at home with the staff's help in the last months of his life. We had beautiful conversations, support from the community, and, in the end, I was there with him, holding his hand.

My father's death was peaceful and loving, and I was grateful for the experience. His choice for end-of-life care had provided me with some direction and preparation, but after he was gone, "normal" never materialized. I found myself very much alone in the world, and with a lot to process. In some ways, I felt like my teen self all over again: While my peers enjoyed their post-college lives, exploring young adulthood and experimenting with relationships and career paths, I found myself riddled with existential anxiety and persistent grief over my multiple losses.

It took me many years to find my way out of the place those early losses had thrust me. I had to battle through a slew of toxic relationships and substance abuse before I found therapy, yoga, meditation, and a sense of purpose. When I finally got there, I was so moved by the process that I decided to become a therapist myself. It was during my master's education when I finally began to piece together the puzzle of my trauma. Losing my parents and struggling to grieve my losses had caused me to develop the anxiety and sadness that had plagued me for so long. I now know that although we can never truly prepare to lose someone we love, there are ways we can better face the end of a life and help us say goodbye. There are also ways we can accept death that will ease the grief process and help us prepare for grief anxiety.

After I earned my master's degree, my first job was for a newly formed hospice organization, and I took on dual roles as the bereavement counselor and the volunteer coordinator. I sat with patients who were facing the end of their lives and families who were grieving the loss of loved ones. I also trained volunteers from the community to provide support for end of life.

Before I began to do this work, I thought I knew a lot about grief—both my parents had died, after all. However, working with the other hospice providers and sitting with families and patients helped me to see grief in a more dimensional way. As I started to understand aspects of anxiety, anger, guilt, depression, trauma, and spirituality from profoundly new perspectives, my love for this work deepened. So did my respect for it. I became a wife and a young mother during those years, and I was often struck by the juxtaposition between the effort we put into bringing a person into the world and the lack of support we offer to those who are making their way out.

After four years, I left the hospice and went into private practice as a therapist, and it was there where my work truly bloomed. When my first book, a memoir about grief, was published, it brought clients through my door on a regular basis. I started to work with all kinds of loss; not only did I work with clients dealing with terminal illness but also murder, suicide, accidents, substance abuse, and even more nuanced forms of loss like abandonment and mental illness. Again, the dimensions of grief expanded for me even more.

I'm not a conventional grief therapist. My style is deeply personal and has always oriented toward the individual. I've always been open about my personal experiences with grief, both on the page and in the room, because I've found that while grief is unique to each person who experiences it, it is also an experience that is difficult to comprehend until you have been through it yourself. My clients seek me out because they know I understand grief on both a personal *and* professional level. They feel comfortable exploring their fears and worries about how they are processing loss because they know that I have experienced these things for myself.

While therapists, mental health experts, and members of the medical community have uncovered extensive information about grief, the field and the interventions are ever-changing. I'm profoundly grateful to all who have studied grief and loss, as well as those who have worked hard to help others understand their various manifestations. But there is always more to learn and more to impart. I'm open to unconventional modalities and treatments, and I'm happy to help someone explore any method that might bring them peace and forward movement in their grief process. We never get over the people we lose, but we *can* learn to live in the world and create meaningful lives in spite of, and sometimes because of, their deaths.

There have been many times in my life when I have wished that I could take on someone's grief and alleviate the pain of their suffering. However, as therapists and mental health care professionals, the most we can do is walk beside our clients down their own path, helping to carry the burden of their loss until they are strong enough to carry the load on their own. My hope is that this book provides the tools for you to support your clients as they become strong.

INTRODUCTION

Fear is a natural reaction to moving closer to the truth.

—Pema Chödrön

Grief and anxiety are inextricably linked. We experience anxiety after a loss because losing someone we love thrusts us into a vulnerable place. It changes our day-to-day lives. It forces us to confront our mortality. Facing these fundamental human truths about life's unpredictability causes fear and anxiety to surface in profound ways.

And yet, this understandable symptom of grief has not been widely explored or recognized until very recently.

The majority of grief literature available today adheres to an old model of grief, revolving around the five stages. And while most of us know the stages—denial, anger, bargaining, depression, acceptance—what many of us don't know is that Elisabeth Kübler-Ross created these stages to help individuals who were facing death themselves, not to address the grief of those left behind. Ross later applied those same stages to the bereaved, but the truth is that they do not adequately cover the grief process. They leave out an essential stage: anxiety.

This overlooked issue is desperate for attention. New clients appear on my couch every week, experiencing debilitating anxiety related to loss. Their symptoms range from full-blown panic attacks and hypochondria to sleep disorders and social phobias. Many cite my book, *Anxiety: The Missing Stage of Grief,* as one of the only resources that pops up after a cursory internet search of "grief + anxiety," and they file into my office one after another, relieved to have found someone who recognizes their plight.

Every experience I've had, both personally and professionally, has led me to the writing of this book. It aims to help clinicians understand why anxiety is so commonly brought on by loss. It is intended for any clinician who is working with clients who are experiencing loss (in all forms), grappling with anxiety surrounding death, and looking for meaning behind the bigger picture of their lives.

ABOUT THIS BOOK

I've given a lot of thought to how to translate the work I do with my clients into a valuable resource for clinicians. Each client you will meet brings their own story of loss and their own unique experience of grief. Everything about who they are in the world and the life they have lived adds a layer of complexity to what they are going through. Although this means that grief looks different for each person who carries it, the common characteristics of grief offer many opportunities for therapeutic support.

I know, firsthand, that the grief process can feel terribly isolating. I also know that it is easier with support. Finding people who can understand what we're going through and who can help us navigate the terrain of loss is vital to the healing process.

You are reading this book because you want to better support your grieving clients. For that, I thank you. The grief process is a lonely journey that every person must ultimately complete, at some point, alone. However, you can support the griever, walking alongside them and helping to carry the weight of their loss. By choosing to work with those who are grieving, you have chosen to bear witness to difficult experiences and to express compassionate support in response to immense vulnerability. Your choice helps the griever, but it also helps to create a broader culture of care and empathy.

HOW TO USE THIS BOOK

This book will expand your toolbox for working with clients suffering from a loss. Included are a number of practical applications, worksheets, exercises, questions, meditations, and the ultimate message that facing death actually helps us to live a fuller life. It can be used alone, as a guide for you in your client work, or in tandem with a grieving person, in and outside of session. My advice is to let your clients guide the pace, giving them ample time and space to process the material—however you choose to present it.

While the grief process plays out differently for everyone, there are stages, phases, and moments that often occur before others, and I have ordered this book with that in mind. That said, for some people, grief can also manifest as a more idiosyncratic process. Consequently, the book can be consulted front to back, or according to clinician or client interest or need. If something jumps out at you, or if there is a particular issue about which you need more information, the book can serve as a valuable resource.

Regardless of your engagement, you'll note that anxiety is my recurring theme. Experience has shown me that anxiety is a major component of grief. Even if clients are not anxious, everything in this book is designed to help them explore, understand, and heal their grief. Additionally, while this book is written specifically to the experience of working with adults, there is plenty here to adapt for work with children and adolescents, and I will leave that up to the clinician's discretion.

My hope is that this book helps you as you help others. It is a privilege to walk with grieving clients on their journeys. As you do so, I urge you to lean into the grief—learn from it, let it transform you, and use that knowledge to inform your support.

CHAPTER 1
SERVING AS A COMPANION TO GRIEF

There are losses that rearrange the world. Deaths that change the way you see everything, grief that tears everything down. Pain that transports you to an entirely different universe, even while everyone else thinks that nothing has really changed.

—**Megan Devine, LPC**

My parents' simultaneous cancer diagnoses when I was 14 years old shrunk my already small world even further. While my friends and classmates explored the new freedoms of adolescence, I accompanied my parents on what felt like an endless rollercoaster ride of hospitals, waiting rooms, and treatments. My mother died five years later, and though my family members and friends were also affected by her passing, I felt utterly bereft in this enormous loss. I was completely unprepared for the many ways grief would manifest.

One day, we will all become familiar with this kind of loss and grief. But despite the universal experience of death, we are not all capable of serving as a companion to grief. I know from firsthand experience that witnessing the pain of others can be wrenching. It's not always easy or intuitive to know what kind of support to offer, or how and when to offer it. And too often, those who are experiencing loss and grief must go through it alone.

Fortunately, I found a therapist to support me in my grief. I gained many valuable things from therapy. Most importantly, I learned that therapists and mental health professionals are uniquely suited to serve as companions to grief. Their specialized training prepares them to accompany others in their pain and provides them the tools to support their clients' nuanced challenges. Further, many therapists and mental health professionals (myself included), feel called to grief work by their own experiences of loss and with a deep desire to help others on grief's journey.

Even for therapists and mental health professionals, however, being a companion to grief poses challenges. It requires compassion, patience, and a willingness to be open. You must be open to the experience of others but also to your own experiences. It isn't easy, but it is fulfilling. When I'm asked if working with grieving clients makes me sad, I'm able to answer honestly that, most of the time, it doesn't. I'm honored to serve in this role. After traveling through grief's painful landscape, I know that a companion can be critical to closure. I also know that grief and loss can offer invaluable wisdom about life and love.

In this chapter, I explain what it means for therapists and mental health professionals to serve as a companion to grief. I discuss grief work, describe what clinicians can expect in this role, introduce the necessary skills, and suggest strategies to mitigate some of the difficulties associated with supporting grieving clients. I also help readers prepare for the challenges of serving as a companion to grief by developing a self-care plan.

PREPARING TO SERVE AS A COMPANION TO GRIEF

Therapists and mental health professionals who specialize in loss and grief often bring profoundly personal experiences to their work. I know I do. It's often *why* we do what we do. Many of us have walked our own path of grief, and we feel called to support others on their journeys. This personal experience means that we approach our clients in ways that differ from that of a traditional psychotherapist. For instance, therapists who work with grieving clients may self-disclose more personal experiences to support clients and help them feel less alone.

However, simply having these personal experiences of loss are not adequate preparation for the challenges associated with grief work. Grief and the pain of loss follow a reasonably predictable course, but symptoms, memories, and can manifest in the most unpredictable ways. Supporting your clients as they express their pain and speak about their grief journey can trigger emotions and unresolved feelings within you, and you must prepare for these potential difficulties.

By caring for yourself, you can better care for your clients, and your preparation for this work is a form of care. In this section, I provide important preparatory information about grief work, including information about self-disclosure and boundary-setting, the team approach to grief work, the short-term nature of grief work, and the issues surrounding terminating grief work.

QUESTIONS FOR THERAPISTS AND MENTAL HEALTH PROFESSIONALS

Think about your personal experiences with loss and grief:

- What formative experiences with loss have you had?
- What have you learned from your experiences of loss and grief that may be applicable to your client work?
- What do you think will challenge you in this work?
- What skills do you have that will help you?
- What skills would you like to acquire?

HANDLING SELF-DISCLOSURE AND BOUNDARY-SETTING

Grief work can differ from traditional psychotherapy in terms of disclosure and boundaries. As I mentioned earlier, many therapists who work in the field of loss and grief come to it from a very personal place of having experienced their own loss. Because grief is not something you can solely understand from a textbook or class, having experienced your own grief is an advantage to serving as a companion to grief.

Of course, your personal knowledge of loss and grief can and should inform your care, but loss and grief are also highly variable and nuanced. Your own experiences provide you with specialized context and insight, but to best support your clients, you must continually reflect on and learn from the many different forms of grief that manifest across the spectrum of human experience.

When working with grieving clients, you might self-disclose more often or set boundaries that differ from those typically set in traditional psychotherapy. For example, you might:

- Acknowledge to your client that you have experienced your own loss(es).

- Allow and encourage your client to share photos and videos of their loved one.

- Attend funerals and memorials.

- Acknowledge difficult dates and anniversaries outside of sessions.

- Conduct joint sessions with partners or family members to help them understand how to support your client or process difficulties in the grief experience.

As you make decisions about boundaries and self-disclosure, repeatedly ask yourself if these approaches are beneficial to the client. There are times when you may feel inclined to share because you relate to something a client is saying or feeling, but if doing so does not directly serve the client, then it is best to refrain and simply continue to bear witness to their journey.

ESTABLISHING A TEAM APPROACH

I have frequently found that working with grieving clients is most effectively supported through a team approach. The more support clients feel they have, the less alone they may feel. I learned this when I was grieving—it wasn't only the therapy that helped me. It was the yoga and the meditation too.

For therapists and mental health professionals, sharing the role of grief companion with a variety of supportive professionals can enhance the effects of counseling and alleviate some of the potential stressors involved in grief work. For these and other reasons, you might find it helpful to establish a strong support network in the form of:

- Psychiatrists

- Physicians

- Nutritionists

- Massage therapists
- Caregiver support
- Funeral and memorial planners
- Spiritual or religious advisers
- Death doulas

You might also find additional support in the form of:
- Grief groups
- Grief retreats
- Yoga
- Sound baths
- EMDR therapy
- Psychedelic therapy
- Art therapy
- Cognitive behavioral therapy
- Trauma counseling

IMPLEMENTING SHORT-TERM THERAPY

Grief therapy is often considered short-term therapy. I usually see clients for an average of six months to one year. This is quite normal for this kind of work. While therapy inevitably encompasses all aspects of a client's life, once they feel more grounded in their grief process, they often feel comfortable moving on from therapeutic support—this moment will occur, of course, at a different time for every client.

Regardless of the length of time I see clients, I always leave the door open for them to come back down the road, even years later. You might consider this as well. Big life experiences, such as divorce, marriage, parenthood, or another loss, tend to reactivate old grief and create a desire for more support. Many clients will also want to come back to see you when they are going through an experience that asks them to reflect on their original loss. Like me, you may relish this opportunity to reconnect and grow.

MANAGING TERMINATION

Terminating with grieving clients is a very delicate process. Because they have been through immense loss, the end of therapy can represent even more loss, and thus, create further grief.

However, termination is also an opportunity to model a healthy and healing goodbye. To facilitate a therapeutic termination, you may want to consider engaging in one or more of the following activities:

- In your early sessions with your clients, co-create a plan with an end date for termination. Knowing the time horizon can help your clients externalize a cycle of healing.

- During your final sessions with clients, take time to reflect on their grief journey over the course of your work together. By helping them reflect on their journey's different stages, they can begin to see their work in therapy as another necessary and useful stage.

- Take time to explicitly process with your clients all the ways that they've grown. Grief work can be painful and upsetting, but it is also a healing process and contains moments of joy. Encourage clients to articulate and honor the changes they've experienced during their grief work.

- Co-create a plan for extended support that includes self-care, family and community support, and other modalities such as a grief group or spiritual care.

- Look ahead with clients to potentially difficult dates, holidays, and anniversaries. Discuss a plan for how they will approach those days and cope with the feelings that will arise.

- Set aside time during your final sessions to reflect on your relationship together. Together, you and your clients have walked the path of grief. Acknowledging and honoring the relationship between the two of you can help to bring closure.

- Be aware that unlike more traditional psychotherapy settings, giving gifts to clients, such as a journal, candle, or something else that will serve as a token of their healing experience, can be appropriate (but is certainly not required).

WHAT TO EXPECT: BEING A COMPANION TO GRIEF

In addition to your personal experiences, you will likely approach grief work with a variety of prior training and clinical experiences. Grieving clients share many characteristics in common with your other clients, but the context of grief therapy might differ from other contexts. Regardless, when working with grieving clients, you can expect to call on a variety of different skills, some old and practiced and some new.

SKILLS FOR SERVING AS A COMPANION TO GRIEF

The skills that follow will be familiar to all practicing therapists and mental health professionals, but they are often used discretely in a typical psychotherapy session. By consciously adopting and practicing these skills as a related set for grief work, you can provide your clients with strong, continuous support.

The companion in grief skill set includes:

- Expressing curiosity rather than experience

- Honoring feelings rather than intellect

- Learning instead of teaching

- Walking alongside instead of leading

- Finding value in silence

- Listening with compassion

- Being empathic and attuned

- Being present

- Bearing witness

- Being willing to go deep

- Setting aside judgment

- Being able to confront personal fear and prejudice

- Being committed to the journey

Some of the most important skills on this list include attunement and empathy. Of course, these traits are valuable skills for everyone, but they are critical for therapists and mental health professionals. Further, these skills may be particularly useful as a companion in grief because grieving clients typically experience a maelstrom of emotions and feelings. They may feel that their emotions are out of their control, or they may feel unable to communicate their emotions and feelings. They require a responsive and compassionate listener to help them focus on and understand their own experiences.

Attunement and empathy also enable therapists and mental health professionals to assume a deep and abiding curiosity about the grieving process. When you lead with curiosity rather than with your experience or expertise, you ensure that you act as a nonjudgmental listener. In fact, leading with curiosity allows you to choose the role of student rather than teacher. As your clients' student, don't attempt to teach them what it means to grieve or how they should expect to feel in their grief. Instead, ask your clients to teach you how it feels and what it means for them to grieve.

In your role as student, you will also become a compassionate witness to your clients' emotions and experiences. You will set aside—and help clients to set aside—any preconceptions about the so-called "correct" or standard way to grieve. You may even need to encourage them to go deeper into their feelings and experiences, regardless of whether those feelings and experiences match working models of the grieving process.

The skill set is mutually reinforcing, but like any skill set, it requires practice. By committing to acquiring and expressing the these skills, you communicate your commitment to being present for your clients as they walk their own paths toward closure.

CHALLENGES TO BEING A COMPANION TO GRIEF

Although I find my work deeply fulfilling, I've found that if I'm not taking proper care to process the stories I hear in my office, I may experience anxiety or lingering sadness. Therapists and mental health professionals are trained to manage any countertransference, but each of us are also a human being. It can be difficult to hear the details of deaths due to excruciating illnesses, terrible accidents, or violent murders. It can be even more difficult to hear these details when they are refracted through the prism of your clients' pain.

Secondary traumatic stress, which can occur with exposure to others who have gone through trauma, is common among therapists and mental health professionals who work with loss and grief. The stress results from the emotional duress that follows from hearing about clients' firsthand trauma experience. Yet, bearing witness to client trauma is a key skill in grief work, and avoiding this exposure is impossible.

This is why it is so important to be aware of this challenging aspect of grief counseling and to prepare to support yourself through the experience of serving as a companion to grief. Such preparation includes encountering and processing your emotions, identifying and practicing self-care techniques, and developing a self-care plan.

ENCOUNTERING AND PROCESSING EMOTIONS

Your clients and their stories will bring up your own grief, sadness, stress, and other emotions. However, you simply cannot help others if you are overwhelmed by your own emotions or impacted by secondary traumatic stress. To prepare for encountering and processing these emotions, it is absolutely necessary to:

- Know your triggers.

- Honor your feelings.

- Find appropriate outlets.

- Refer out when necessary.

- Identify self-care techniques.

- Develop a self-care plan.

To be ready for potential overwhelm, it is critical to *know your triggers*. You are likely already familiar with your triggers, as training and professional experience frequently lead you to encounter them. But some client stories or behaviors will provoke painful or difficult-to-ignore emotions and feelings. Take a moment to reflect on client personalities, stories, or contexts that typically provoke these emotions for you. How might grieving clients provoke these—and other—triggers?

_____

_____

_____

_____

Your triggers typically bring up challenging emotions and feelings. Consequently, you must *anticipate difficult feelings*, welcoming and honoring them in order to process them. You can welcome your feelings by making space for them, by holding them up to the light, and by naming them. You can honor your feelings not by judging them but by validating them. Your difficult feelings have a right to exist and to be felt. Consider the emotions and feelings that typically arise for you when you feel triggered. How will you welcome these feelings and honor them?

_____

_____

_____

_____

To process your feelings, you must *find proper outlets for those feelings*. Being a companion to grief means hearing heartbreaking stories of death every day. These are not stories that can be easily shared with another mental health professional for fear of causing secondary trauma. To prepare for the challenge of finding a proper outlet for your feelings, consider the support networks and professionals you already call on. Within this group, identify some contacts, possibly those who work in the field of loss and grief, that can form a support network for grief work. How will you lean on the members of this network, and what other networks or relationships can you begin to establish?

_____

_____

_____

_____

While it is important to display compassion to grieving clients, it is also important to *avoid displays of difficult emotions or releases of emotion*. This is one of the reasons it is so necessary to know your triggers and to anticipate and process difficult feelings. The preparatory and processing work you do will help you to save any displays and releases of emotion for outside of sessions. Think about the strong emotions you associate with your triggers. How do you navigate those emotions? How do you deal with them when they arise during session? How can you attend to these emotions outside of session?

_____

_____

_____

_____

Sometimes clients—or their stories—will provoke a response that is especially difficult to process. To prepare for this eventuality, it is necessary to *find support and supervision for cases that are overwhelming.* You already know that this is a role that can't be filled by just anyone. Consider the professional resources you have or can locate to support and supervise you as you act as a companion to grief. How will you seek out this support and supervision? Will you integrate support and supervision into each case, or will it depend on the case? How will you know that you need support and supervision?

_____

_____

_____

_____

A network of support is vital, but it is not always enough. If you serve as a companion to grief, you must be able to *recognize when to refer out the cases that you know you are unable to handle.* As you think about future client work, how will you know when it is time to refer a client? What referral network can you establish now to ensure your grieving clients are supported when you are unable to provide support?

_____

_____

_____

_____

It is much more difficult to fulfill any of these obligations without knowing the self-care techniques that support your work and without implementing a self-care plan to ensure you're taking care of yourself in this incredibly fulfilling but very challenging work.

IDENTIFYING SELF-CARE TECHNIQUES

Putting a plan in place for processing the emotions and feelings associated with being a companion to grief is a big part of self-care. But therapists and mental health care professionals must practice self-care techniques every single day. Such activities do not necessarily depend on client work and should instead be integrated into each day as a matter of course. The activities listed in this section can help to strengthen regulation and ensure that you are fully present—first to yourself—and then to your grieving clients.

Some self-care activities may seem mundane, and, in a way, they are. Yet how many of us truly prioritize these exercises? How many of us practice one or more of these self-care techniques every single day? Despite knowing that self-care is critical to our well-being, and consequently to our patient care, many of us deprioritize what we may see as superfluous *for us*.

However, when approaching loss and grief, it is absolutely necessary to consider self-care a foundational element of client care. Choose a handful of the following activities that you know you can complete as part of an effective routine. Then, create a plan to ensure their completion.

Activities for self-care may include:

- Journaling
- Exercising
- Meditating
- Relaxing
- Making time for joy and pleasure
- Spending time in nature
- Doing body work
- Receiving acupuncture
- Recognizing your limits for your workload
- Seeing a therapist, support network, or supervisor

CREATING SELF-CARE PLANS

To support your completion of your self-care plan, commit to specific plans and guidelines. Reflect on the following questions, and use the information you find to write up your own self-care plan.

What are the ways you currently take care of yourself before and after work?

_____

_____

_____

How effective are these methods?

_____

_____

_____

What new ways would you like to try?

_____

_____

_____

With whom can you process your cases?

_____

_____

_____

With whom can you make a *regular* date to process your cases?

_____

_____

_____

What signs tell you that you are reaching your burnout or overwhelm limit?

_____

_____

_____

What signals tell you that you are working too much?

_____

_____

_____

When will you check in with yourself to ensure you are not reaching overwhelm?

_____

_____

_____

How do you allocate for time off if needed?

_____

_____

_____

What can you add to your life to bring you joy and pleasure?

_____

_____

_____

QUESTIONS FOR THERAPISTS AND MENTAL HEALTH PROFESSIONALS

As you prepare yourself for the work of being a companion to grief, answer these questions, providing as much detail as possible. After each chapter, and whenever you feel you are struggling or questioning your work, revisit these questions and revise your answers:

- Why do you want to do grief work?
- What do you expect grief work to be like?
- What do you look forward to in this work?
- What do you fear or worry about with this work?
- What do you need to do to feel prepared for this work?

REFLECTION

Although it isn't always easy to be a companion to grief, the rewards of the work make the hardships so worth it. In acting as this companion, you are answering a call, and in doing so, you have the singular honor of acting as a guide to terrain that many people know all too well. Very few people are comfortable navigating this territory. But you can, and because you can, you must. I hope your work with grieving clients is as rewarding as my own has been. I believe that in doing this work, we honor the loved ones who have died and expand the lives of those still living.

CHAPTER 2

LISTENING TO THE STORY OF LOSS

There is no greater agony than bearing an untold story inside you.

—Maya Angelou

I went into my first session with a grief counselor knowing very little about the process of therapy. I remember being surprised by how cathartic it was to pour out my story to my therapist—all the memories, pain, and confusion I'd been holding inside for so many years. I also found it profoundly healing to experience the ability of my therapist to hold space for my story, to bear witness to my experience, and to listen to me in a way that no one ever had.

When clients come to you because they are grieving, your first task is to support them as they tell you about their loss. Many clients often long to tell their story. They ache to release the feelings, however difficult it may be. But a large number of clients will still feel anxious about telling it. The anxiety may be attributed to different reasons. Often, grieving clients simply do not have enough outlets for their grief. They can't tell their story of loss to just anyone, nor can they tell their story just anywhere. They may consequently arrive at their first session with you as I did with my own therapist: not knowing how to talk about what I'd gone through.

I know from my own experience that telling the story of loss for the first time and in a safe place can be a cathartic and healing experience. It can also be crucial to the grieving process. Over the course of work with a grieving client, they will share their story of loss multiple times and through multiple lenses as they work to integrate the story of their loss into the narrative of their entire life.

In this chapter, I will discuss how to prepare to listen to your clients' stories of loss, including how to approach some of the challenges posed by idiomatic expressions of death. I will also explain the general process for actively listening to grieving clients, describe what you should listen for, and point out when you should ask—and refrain from asking—questions. Finally, I will suggest a method to help you process the impact of hearing your clients' stories.

PREPARING TO LISTEN TO THE STORY OF LOSS

While the first session of standard psychotherapy typically features an intake, the first session for a client seeking support for loss and grief must also focus on their story of loss. These stories can take many, and sometimes unexpected, forms.

For instance, if a client's loss is recent, they may want to tell you every painstaking detail that led up to their loved one's death. Some clients with a recent loss may take a different approach and reserve certain painful details for later sessions.

If a client's loss is older, they may not remember everything. They may tell you shortened versions of their loss, or they may struggle, silently or aloud, to remember what they once considered key details.

Some clients express a lot of emotion when telling their story of loss; some express very little. Some may express concern about their story's effect on you, particularly if the death was very sad or very traumatic. Others may forge ahead and share traumatic details regardless of the potential effect. Some clients may not be able to get through their whole story in one session, and some may only feel comfortable telling you a very short version the first time you meet. All of these variations are okay and to be expected.

Stories of loss come in many forms. It's not just that every client has a different story of loss. It's that every client's story includes multiple variations. Over time, details can and will shift depending on clients' proximity to the loss and their changing relationships with their loved one, with themselves, and with you. For this reason, clients will—and must—repeat their stories of loss at different times and from different perspectives as they work through the grieving process and toward closure.

To prepare to listen to these stories, this section offers preparatory information, including the difference between listening to grief stories in the therapeutic setting versus hearing grief stories outside of session, and issues associated with grief terminology.

SHARING GRIEF STORIES IN REAL LIFE

A client's experience of sharing their story of loss in a therapeutic setting will differ significantly from their other experiences of sharing their loss. Typically, their other experiences are characterized by feeling awkward, unheard, rushed, or pressured not to be too sad or too fixated on their loss. Although most people want to be comforting toward someone going through a loss, many can also having trouble hearing and supportively listening.

Faced with the agony of another person's grief, well-meaning people often try to find ways to make the grieving person feel better. They may, for instance, offer solutions to a grieving person who tries to share their story of loss. Or perhaps in an effort to close a difficult conversation, they may offer what, to the grieving person, feels like empty words of comfort. Almost everybody wants to make the grieving person feel better, but these experiences can be hurtful and even harmful to a grieving person.

When a grieving person comes to therapy for support, these real-life experiences may impact the way they initially share their story with you. It may take some time or a few attempts for them to trust that you are able to not only hear their story but to supportively listen to it.

USING GRIEF TERMINOLOGY

Issues associated with grief terminology typically present in the first session, when the client first tells you their story of loss. Clients may refer to their loved one's death in a number of ways, including through the following language:

- Passed away

- Departed

- Lost

- Gone

- Death

- Dying

- Died

- Dead

A school of thought in the world of bereavement continues to suggest that clinicians should use concrete words like *dead*, *death*, *die*, and *dying* to help their clients face the reality of their loss. However, clients commonly use phrases such as *passed away* or refer to their loved one being *gone*.

As with so many other aspects of loss and grief, there is no one-size-fits-all solution. There are times when using gentler euphemisms for death can help soften a conversation or give a grieving person time and space to process the pain of their loss. There are also times when speaking more directly might be a better option.

Then again, different words and phrases mean different things to different people in different contexts. Take the phrase *passed away*: It first appears in English writings in the 1400s, when most people believed that after death the soul physically *passed on* to the afterlife. Today, the phrase has become a euphemism, and as such, it can help some people more comfortably address difficult topics like fear and grief.

When it comes to the most appropriate and supportive terminology, your best approach is a flexible one. In general, I base my own terminology on sensitivity to the client's comfort level. Some clients may privilege euphemism, even though it feels more appropriate for you, in your role as therapist, to use a direct term. If clients use euphemisms, I may refrain from using overtly direct language until they are ready to address the topic more directly. On the other hand, direct terminology such as *died* may be useful when grieving clients need support in reaching a more concrete understanding of the events surrounding their loved one's death.

Some clients may prefer to use very direct—or even harsh terminology—to approach the death of their loved one. Such language may act, for them, as a kind of exposure therapy, inuring them to the shock of their loss. This kind of terminology may not feel appropriate to you as a companion to their grief. If this is the case, you may explore this choice as you see fit, but be sure that the decision is not coming from a place of countertransference.

No matter which terms your clients use, you can directly address their choice of words when appropriate in session. Ask them how it feels to use their chosen words. Such a conversation not only helps them to reflect on their choices, but it can also offer important insight. For example, I once had a client with strong spiritual beliefs explain to me that she preferred to use the phrase *passed over*, not because it gave her a protective way to discuss her loved one's death but because it fit with her belief system.

Whatever terminology you choose, and however you choose to handle the language shared between you and your clients, it's best to do so with curiosity and an open mind.

QUESTIONS FOR THERAPISTS AND MENTAL HEALTH PROFESSIONALS

The words you use are based on a multitude of factors—including your background, past experiences, and who you are talking to. Take a moment to consider the terminology you use when talking about death, dying, and loss:

- What words do you use when discussing death?
- How do those words help you to think about death?
- Do any words about death make you feel uncomfortable? Why?

WHAT TO EXPECT: LISTENING TO THE STORY OF LOSS

As a therapist or mental health professional, you strive to truly listen to all of your clients, and clients coping with loss frequently experience intense relief when they feel their stories have been heard. You can help provide them with this supportive catharsis by creating an inviting environment for them to begin to share their stories and by communicating your willingness to actively listen.

Start by reflecting on your own sense of what makes for an inviting environment. When have you felt most heard? What emotions and feelings were you experiencing? What was your environment like? What was your conversational partner like? What can you do to recreate this environment during sessions?

_____

_____

_____

_____

Then, reflect on some challenging discussions you've had with previous clients. What fears did you experience in anticipation of these conversations? What emotions and feelings did you experience during them? What have you learned from these and other conversations that can prepare you for talking about sad and difficult things?

_____

_____

_____

_____

_____

Your reflections will help to prepare you for the inevitable challenges associated with listening to stories of loss. They will also allow you to focus on the skills that will best help clients to feel heard. In this section, I discuss these skills and supply a general guide for applying these skills, including what to listen for, what questions to ask, how to close the story of loss, and questions to pose to clients to prompt reflection.

INVITING THE STORY OF LOSS

It's useful to approach listening to the story of loss as being part of a process. This process begins when you invite clients to share their story of loss. However, in this context, "inviting" takes on new and different meanings.

You implicitly invite clients to share their story of loss when you provide them with a therapeutic environment and communicate your ability to act as a supportive companion to their grief. You extend this invitation in the first moments of your first session. For instance, you might invite them to start wherever they would like, or you may suggest a particular starting point. You may even acknowledge that you understand that telling their story of loss is an emotional undertaking, and you might reassure them that you are here to support them in this experience. Attending to their potential concerns before they arise can help your clients feel comfortable enough to begin sharing their story.

When it is time for clients to share, extend an explicit invitation and reinforce that invitation by using the following steps as a rough guide:

1. Assure your client that you can handle their story and would like to hear it.

2. Invite them to begin wherever they would like.

3. As they share, listen with appropriate facial expressions and nodding.

4. Only ask leading questions if the client is reticent or struggling to tell their story.

5. When they conclude, thank them for sharing their story.

The steps may seem straightforward, but they require a bit more than meets the eye. As you begin to actively listen to your client's story of loss, particularly in the story's first iteration, it's important to remain as open and nonjudgmental as possible. You can communicate your openness by centering the client and their story. This means maintaining a calm, compassionate demeanor, even if the story is painful to hear. It also means keeping your movements to a minimum so as not to distract the client. For example, you might consider keeping tissues nearby or offering them a beverage before the session's start. This allows the client to easily find comforts without interrupting the story's flow by getting up or taking a long pause.

Centering a client and their story also means allowing them to tell their story unimpeded by verbal interruptions or clarifying questions. It means indicating active listening by nodding in appropriate places and offering compassionate facial expressions. Finally, it means refraining from crying or comforting. Crying and comforting are different impulses, but both tend to relocate the focus from the client to you. In this case, your client may then feel that they need to take care of you, either by providing comfort or assurance that they are okay.

ASKING QUESTIONS

The first time clients share their story of loss, it is important to listen without interrupting with clarifying questions. Your questions may be important—they may even affect your comprehension of their story—but refraining from interruptions will allow you to see how they approach and tell their story without assistance. If, for example, you have a great deal of trouble understanding a client's story, it may indicate that they feel significant overwhelm and may require support, in later retellings, to slow down and access their story of loss in smaller increments.

Once clients have finished their story, or once you've reached a moment of closure, you can ask a question or two to clarify something confusing or understand vital details, if known. Such questions should focus on the important pieces of information that contribute to a deeper understanding of the client's experience of loss. These should be questions that focus on significant fundamental information not likely to change in subsequent retellings. In the case of overwhelmed clients, clients who are reticent, or clients who struggle to tell their story, such questions can also be used as prompts that can help to ease their way. You may ask questions like:

- When did the loss take place?
- How old was the client when the loss occurred?
- How did the loved one die?
- Does anyone have a different version of how the loved one died?

UNDERSTANDING THE STORY OF LOSS

It is natural and expected for stories of loss to change over time, especially when grief is explored and processed in therapy. In clients' repeated retellings of their story, certain elements of their story may become more or less relevant. Details that might initially seem crucial can become less important, and vice versa.

To help assess a client's changing relationship to their story of loss and to gain insight into their grieving process, listen for and take note of the information they provide around the following questions:

- Where does the story begin and end?

- Who are the central figures in the story beside your client and the person they lost?

- Are there certain phrases or words the client frequently uses?

- Are there parts of the story that evoke emotions like anger, anxiety, and sadness for the client?

- Are there places in the story where the client expresses no emotion?

- Are the details concise or blurry?

- Is the story told linearly or does it jump around?

Note that these are not questions that need to be posed to clients because the answers will emerge as they share their stories. However, the answers you discover will help you to identify how clients are managing their grief and how they are integrating their stories of loss into their larger life narratives. The answers will also offer insight into the ways that they relate to the different parts of their stories. As their relationships to their loss change, these answers, and the emotions and feelings associated with them, may change too.

FACILITATING A CONCLUSION

For your clients, concluding their story of loss may be just as difficult, or even more so, than beginning them. Some clients may feel unable or unwilling to conclude their story of loss because it signals an end to the therapeutic experience. Some may be reluctant because it shifts the focus from their loved one to themselves. But although they may feel uncomfortable, helping your clients manage the conclusion of their story allows them to experience healthy closure.

In-session time management constitutes a major part of helping clients to approach their story's conclusion. Many times, clients will not be able to finish their story before the end of a session. If this is the case, it is still necessary to make time to explicitly conclude the session and offer an opportunity for reflection.

This may mean that it is necessary to gently interrupt a client's story to let them know that the session is drawing to an end. It is difficult—both for the client and for you—to interrupt someone who is upset or emotionally dysregulated. Therefore, as the session begins to wind down, work to identify a natural pause within the story where you can suggest a temporary conclusion. Lead your client in a moment of reflection by inviting them to consider how it felt to share their story and how it made them feel about embarking on this journey of grief work.

FOSTERING REFLECTION

From inviting your clients to tell their story, to supporting them as they tell it, to helping them manage its conclusion, listening to their story of loss offers several opportunities for you to help foster integration and closure. Facilitating reflection can stimulate integration and can act as an aid to conclusion. There are many ways to help clients deepen their initial reflections. Consider posing to clients the following suggestions, which they can complete out of session:

- Write your story of loss and note if there are any differences that arise in writing it as opposed to telling it.
- Journal about your expectations for therapy.
- Write yourself a letter about why you are seeking help.
- Think about any parts of the story that you are withholding and consider reasons why you might be withholding them.

QUESTIONS FOR THERAPISTS AND MENTAL HEALTH PROFESSIONALS

As you prepare to listen to stories of loss, it can be helpful to identify potential gaps between your expectations and the realities of your client experiences. Prepare yourself to listen more effectively by answering the following questions:

- How would you like to invite clients to tell their story, and how would you like these stories to unfold?
- How can you prepare yourself for variations that you don't anticipate?
- How can you prepare your clients for the possibility of running out of time before they complete their story?
- Are you comfortable going over time if a client has not finished telling their story?

CHALLENGES OF LISTENING TO A STORY OF LOSS

Most challenges of listening to a client's story of loss are typically confined to difficulties with implementing the skills explained in this chapter. These difficulties often stem from stories of loss that are particularly triggering. However, with appropriate preparation, as discussed in the previous chapter, you will be able to process the emotions that are triggered, call on your support network as needed, and consider referring out in the case of a story or client that challenges your ability to listen effectively.

QUESTIONS FOR THERAPISTS AND MENTAL HEALTH PROFESSIONALS

To navigate the difficulties associated with listening to stories of loss, it's important to stay tuned in to yourself when listening. You can foster this capability by taking time to process client stories through the following questions:

- Were there parts of the story that were triggering for you?
- Did you feel emotional at any point? If so, when?
- Did you feel bored at any point? If so, when?
- Did you feel confused?
- What parts of the story reminded you of your own life?
- What parts of the story gave you anxiety?

REFLECTION

For some people, grief can feel profoundly private. There may be a sense that they must act stoic or hide their grief in public due to the fabricated idea that expressing intense emotions, particularly those associated with loss or despair, is in some way forbidden. Many people feel uncomfortable when witnessing the pain of others. They may want to turn away from the expressions of pain out of a reflexive sense of self-preservation. Motivated perhaps by fear, they want to avoid feeling hurt too.

This collective denial of displays of grief is mutually reinforcing: When someone denies the grief of others, they also deny it in ourselves. For this and many other reasons, it can be very difficult for clients to tell, reflect on, or even think about their story of loss. They may seek support for these activities in therapy, but even after they muster the courage to tell their story, they may not know quite what support they seek.

As a therapist or mental health professional, you are capable of turning toward your clients' painful experiences to act as a supportive companion to grief and an active listener to their emotions and feelings. By fostering a client's reflection on their story of loss, and by helping them to identify what help they hope to receive in therapy, you help them gently externalize their relationship to their loss and identify their needs as they process it.

CHAPTER 3

UNDERSTANDING GRIEF

The only cure for grief is to grieve.

—**Dr. Earl Grollman**

After my mother died, I felt enormous pressure to curtail my grief and move on. After all, my support group then had pushed me in that direction—my friends and family didn't want my sadness to stop me or slow me down. Maybe they thought that if I paused my education, my training, or my social calendar in order to grieve, I might never start living my life again.

I know they only wanted the best for me, but as a result of this belief that I needed to keep going—to continue living my life as though I hadn't lost the most important thing in it—I wasn't able to process my grief. I felt paralyzed, like I couldn't gain enough of a foothold to move forward. The resulting mental atrophy contributed to significant anxiety.

I learned an important lesson from this experience, one that has been reinforced by my work: When clients are unable to grieve, whether from personality or environmental factors, they experience some amount of anxiety and cannot move on. They need to fully grieve their loss to be able to move through the grieving process and find closure.

Helping your clients to approach and understand their own process of grief, however it manifests, will not only enable them to feel all the different elements of their grief, but it will, in turn, alleviate their anxiety. Clients are very often new to the kind of grief they are experiencing. They do not yet understand the dynamics of grief, nor are they familiar with the symptoms of anxiety that can accompany it. Educating clients on the wide range of what's to be expected during the grieving process, and giving them permission to feel things they weren't prepared to feel, is extremely important.

In this chapter, I offer information and tools to help therapists and clients understand and approach the grieving process. In the first part of the chapter, I explain the broad context of grief, including its different types, characteristics, and expressions. I also discuss the major models of grief that inform client care. In the second part, I describe the grieving process from the perspective of the client. Almost every person who has grieved has wondered about their experience of loss. I point out the common and not-so-common emotions and feelings that can accompany the grieving process, as well as the way that time can impact grief and feelings associated with loss.

PREPARING TO UNDERSTAND GRIEF

Not all losses are the same, and not all losses affect people in the same way. The circumstances of each loss can help determine the type of loss, and the type of loss often has some impact on how clients grieve. But as you know, grief is not predictable, and the different types of loss cannot possibly correspond to predictable experiences. These labels do, however, offer a baseline that can help clients understand and relate to their experiences more deeply. Each category of loss may result in different emotions, feelings, and behaviors, as well as different timelines for grief and mourning.

TYPES OF LOSS

While there are many different types of loss, ranging from the death of a loved one to the dissolution of a marriage, or the loss of a job to repeated instances of infertility, the following are different types of loss that involve death, which is often the most ultimate loss of them all:

- **Anticipated loss:** Some clients going through the grieving process know that their loved one is going to die, perhaps because they have received a terminal diagnosis. Despite this foreknowledge, anticipated loss does not lessen grief. Instead, it provokes an earlier start to the grieving process. For instance, a client may begin to grieve when they learn of their loved one's terminal prognosis or at any other point leading up to when their loved one dies.

- **Sudden and unexpected loss:** Some clients going through the grieving process experience the loss of their loved one suddenly or as a shock. When you abruptly lose someone, it is normal to feel disbelief or to feel stunned. An unexpected loss can result in a client moving through their grieving process slowly because their mind and body need to approach and understand what has happened.

- **Traumatic or violent loss:** Traumatic loss occurs when a loved one is violently killed or dies by suicide. A client who experiences the traumatic or violent loss of a loved one feel additional emotions and feelings associated with sudden and unexpected loss. This can complicate their grieving experience with additional layers of shock and grief.

There is a caveat when considering the type of loss and its potential impact on a grieving client: While the type of loss is an important variable in a client's grief, so too is the relationship they shared with their loved one. The degree of closeness, the role the person had in their life, and their feelings for and about them, will likely influence their grief.

This does not mean that there is a definitive correlation between the closeness of a relationship and how strongly a client feels the loss. It simply means that this relationship between client and loved one can impact their experience in their grieving process. All in all, helping your clients approach the grieving process requires an understanding of the clients themselves—as well as their histories.

TYPES OF GRIEF

The type of grief that your clients experience cannot possibly predict how their symptoms, emotions, and experience will manifest, but understanding the general categories of grief—and which of these each client most accurately reflects—can inform the therapist of the support required.

It's also important to keep in mind that while there is a relationship between the type of loss and the type of grief, this relationship is neither particularly obvious nor especially straightforward. For instance, a client may experience typical grief after losing a child in a traumatic way, while another client could experience unexpectedly complicated grief after the anticipated loss of a family member whom they were not especially close. The following broad categories help characterize grief's different variations and suggest opportunities for client education:

- **Typical grief:** Typical grief is generally considered to be the natural grief that arises due to the loss of a person. This grief encompasses a range of emotions including sorrow, distress, anger, and anxiety. "Typical" refers to the common and expected emotions, feelings, and behaviors associated with the death of a loved one. Naturally, clients do not experience their grief as "typical." Most clients, even those who have experienced anticipatory loss, experience their grief instead as atypical irruptions in their previously whole lives.

- **Ambiguous grief:** Ambiguous grief follows a loss that lacks closure, information, and resolution. It's the kind of grief that comes with divorce, breakups, estrangement, and adoption: The person you are grieving is still alive, but you are disconnected due to various circumstances. This grief is "ambiguous" because the relationship still has possible potential.

- **Disenfranchised grief:** Disenfranchised grief is grief that is not widely recognized or acknowledged by society. This grief extends to pregnancy loss, infertility, racism, and many of the other less obvious losses such as retirement, pet loss, moves, and seasons of life. When your community does not value or recognize your feelings of grief over such losses, your feelings may not be validated and your experience is minimized.

- **Anticipatory grief:** Anticipatory grief is the experience of the feelings that arise when you are facing a loss in the future. It could be the loss of a person, a pet, a house, a job, a marriage, or even a body part. When you know you are going to lose someone or something, you anticipate the pain of that loss. Anticipatory grief is often accompanied by anxiety, as you face uncertainty regarding *when* you will experience the loss.

- **Complicated grief:** Complicated grief is an extended process of grieving with debilitating, persistent, and intense emotions that impact your engagement with life as a whole. Complicated grief occurs when you experience traumatic loss, when you lose someone with whom you had a complex relationship, or when your environment or circumstances exacerbate your ability to cope. In some ways, all grief is complicated, but some people will have more layers to work through than others.

WHAT TO EXPECT: UNDERSTANDING GRIEF

There is no predictive model through which a client's grief can be fully understood. Consequently, there is no one way to grieve. Grieving people often experience pressure around grieving in the "right" way. Some of this pressure is the result of the aberrant experience of grief itself. For some people, this experience may be the first time in their lives that they have come across this kind of emotional turbulence. The experience differs so much from their expectations that they sometimes assume they must be doing it wrong. But just as there is no *one* way to grieve, there is no *right* way to grieve. This is perhaps the most important piece of information that therapists and mental health professionals can impart to their grieving clients.

In fact, even when a client's experience of grief appears to exactly replicate one of the models of grief—that we will touch on later in this chapter—your client's individuality, the individuality of their loved one who has died, the specificity of their relationship to one another, and the singularity of their particular experience of loss can manifest in their grieving process in different, and perhaps unexpected, ways.

QUESTIONS FOR THERAPISTS AND MENTAL HEALTH PROFESSIONALS

We all have preconceptions informing our ideas of grief. Take a moment to consider your own ideas about what constitutes so-called typical grief:

- What are your ideas about what grief is supposed to look like?
- What informed these ideas? Do these ideas reflect any biases?
- How can you expand your awareness to include aspects of grief you have not previously recognized or considered? (e.g., types of loss, types of grief, common presentations of grief, models of grief)
- After reflecting on the utility of the models you use in your grief work, can you design a model of grief that you think could be helpful to one of the clients you are supporting?

UNDERSTANDING WHAT GRIEF LOOKS LIKE

Regardless of circumstances, your clients will present in session with a wide variety of emotions, feelings, behaviors, and even physical symptoms associated with their grieving process. Clients may anticipate some of these emotions and feelings—for instance, few clients are surprised when they cry after the death of a loved one. But some may become confused or even alarmed when less expected experiences transpire, such as feelings of numbness, excessive sleeping, or heart palpitations.

Your ability to explain and contextualize the broad range of emotions, feelings, behaviors, and physical symptoms by which grief makes itself known will go a long way toward approaching what, to your clients, is a new and unwelcome experience. The following list describes some, though not all, expressions of grief.

Crying • Numbness • Anxiety • Forgetfulness • Feeling unhinged • Anger • Insomnia • Excessive sleeping • Frustration • Confusion • Loneliness • Fear • Inability to talk to friends • Inability to stop talking to friends • Inability to be alone • Inability to be with others • Laughing • Screaming • Inability to eat or uninterested in eating • Eating or wanting to eat all the time • Inability to go to work • Escaping into work • Not enjoying things you used to love • Memory loss • Inability to connect with reality • Stomachaches • Sobbing on the floor • Feeling nothing • Experiencing dreams or nightmares • Restlessness • Heart palpitations • Fear of or worry over imminent death • Fear of or worry over other people's imminent death • Wanting to look through photos and remember memories • Not wanting to look through photos or remember memories • More crying • More numbness • Feeling lost • Feeling scared

---

APPROACHING MAJOR MODELS OF GRIEF

Regardless of their reactions to grief, all of a client's experiences cohere into their grieving process. This process differs for each client according to the many variables affecting their grief. However, their particular process can often be more deeply understood through one or more of the major models of grief. Again, no one model or theory of loss will perfectly fit any client's situation, but models and theories offer a useful context for your work.

In fact, clients are frequently drawn to these models of grief and the descriptions of stages and phases they offer. This should not be surprising. People generally seek patterns to order life's events, and grieving people often yearn for a formula to understand their pain. *If only I could just go through these five stages, then I would feel better*, they might think. But, of course, grief doesn't work like that. Part of your work is to help clients understand that each experience of grief is particular unto itself.

Educating clients about theories and models of grief can also be fraught. Sometimes, when clients learn about a particular theory or model, they try to fit themselves into it. As they navigate unpredictable emotions and feelings, they may end up feeling even more lost than when they first sought support. I can't tell you how many clients have come to my office exclaiming that they must be doing something wrong because they are not grieving in the way that is suggested by one or more theories. Therefore, you should use the models as guideposts, and work with only what feels useful to you and to each individual client. The following are synopses of some of the most prominent frameworks for grief that I use in my work.

Elisabeth Kübler-Ross's Five Stages of Grief

The five stages of grief is the most well-known of all the grief models. It was coined by Swiss physician Elisabeth Kübler-Ross in 1969. Most people now know that the stages were originally intended as a framework for what a terminally ill person experiences when they are facing death, but the stages were later applied to the grief process as well. Kübler-Ross's five stages of grief are:

- **Denial:** In this stage, the grieving person has difficulty comprehending the reality of the loss. It takes time to wrap their head around what has happened. They may believe there has been a mistake, refuse to acknowledge the loss, continue to speak about their loved one in the present tense, or even pretend that their loved one is coming back soon.

- **Anger:** This stage refers to the anger that arises following a loss. The anger can manifest in everything from general irritability to self-blame. The grieving person might even feel targeted anger at specific individuals.

- **Bargaining:** In this stage, if-only thoughts arise after the loss. The grieving person frequently ruminates on ways that things could have been different.

- **Depression:** This stage includes sadness, hopelessness, despair, and fatigue. While it's common for a grieving person to feel all of these things after a loss, sometimes they need help moving through them, particularly if their day-to-day functioning becomes severely impaired.

- **Acceptance:** This stage may be a misnomer. The grieving person does not feel suddenly over their loss or at peace with it. Instead, they have accepted the reality of their loss and are finding ways to incorporate it into their life.

Sigmund Freud's Theory of Mourning

Sigmund Freud was the first to suggest a theory for how people should move through grief. He suggested that the grieving person may first allow themselves to grieve and find ways to express their pain, but then they must make efforts to emotionally detach themselves from the person they lost.

When Freud later lost his 26-year-old daughter, Sophie, he did not fulfill his theory of mourning. He admitted that the pain and emptiness he felt over this loss would never leave him. He acknowledged that it may weaken over time but that there was nothing that would erase it altogether. In fact, nine years after the loss, in a letter to Ludwig Binswanger, Freud wrote that he still hadn't been able to come to terms with the experience. Freud finally came to understand that the bond we have with our loved ones shouldn't be abandoned, as it is our way of holding onto them after they are gone.

Erich Lindemann's Grief Work Theory

Erich Lindemann was a German American writer, psychiatrist, and grief specialist who built on Freud's work by developing three tasks that help grieving people process and recover from their grief. As the author of a paper entitled "Symptomatology and Management of Acute Grief," he was particularly interested in posttraumatic stress. According to Lindemann, the three tasks of grieving people include:

- Emancipating their bondage to the deceased

- Readjusting to a new environment where the deceased is missing

- Forming new relationships

Lindemann coined the term "grief work" during his work with grieving survivors of the 1942 Cocoanut Grove fire. His research is often cited as some of the earliest work that revealed the long-term impact of grief and trauma, and he went on to influence both Kübler-Ross and John Bowlby.

Lindemann was particularly interested in understanding the symptomology of grief. The most common symptoms he noted include:

- **Somatic distress:** difficulty breathing, loss of appetite, exhaustion

- **Preoccupation with the deceased:** a fixation on specific images, difficult memories, and also positive reflections of the person who died

- **Guilt:** the perception that the grieving person could have or should have done something to prevent the death

- **Hostile reactions:** the expression of irritability and anger toward others

- **Loss of pattern of conduct:** changes to regular functioning including restlessness, feelings of meaninglessness, and lack of motivation

John Bowlby and Colin Murray Parkes's Four Stages of Grief

John Bowlby was a British psychologist and psychiatrist who pioneered attachment theory, which looks at how our early bonds affect our relationships throughout life. He noted that grief is a normal, adaptive response to loss, given that the "affectional-bond" has been broken. He and his colleague, Colin Murray Parkes, broke down this adaptive grief response into four phases of grief:

- **Shock and numbness:** In this phase, the grieving person feels that the loss isn't real and experiences somatic distress.

- **Yearning and searching:** The phase is characterized by a longing and searching for the person who is gone as the grieving individual becomes aware of the void that has been left in their life.

- **Despair and disorganization:** In this phase, the grieving person accepts that life will not be the same, and this acceptance is accompanied by feelings of despair and hopelessness.

- **Reorganization and recovery:** In this phase, day-to-day functioning improves and faith in the future is restored.

William Worden's Four Tasks of Grief

In William Worden's book *Grief Counseling and Grief Therapy*, he suggests that grieving individuals must accomplish four tasks for "the process of mourning to be completed" and "equilibrium to be reestablished." Although Worden makes clear these are in no particular order, there is a natural order because the completion of some tasks presuppose completion of other tasks. He acknowledges that people may need to revisit certain tasks over time, that grief is not linear, and that it is difficult to determine a timeline for completing tasks associated with grief. Worden's four tasks include:

- Accepting the reality of the loss

- Processing pain and grief

- Adjusting to the world without the loved one

- Finding a way to maintain a connection with the loved one

Therese Rando's Six Rs of Bereavement

Therese Rando, an American clinical psychologist and the author of *How to Go On Living When Someone Dies*, has published many articles and consulted on many media presentations to talk about her theory of grief. According to her theory, three phases of mourning encompass six different processes:

- Avoidance Phase

  1. Recognize the loss: Acknowledge and understand the death.

- Confrontation Phase

  2. React to the separation: Experience the pain and emotional responses to the loss.

  3. Recollect and reexperience the deceased: Review and remember the deceased.

  4. Relinquish the old attachment: Relinquish the world where you were accustomed to your loved one's presence.

- Accommodation Phase

  5. Readjust to a new world: Move adaptively into this new world without forgetting the old one.

  6. Reinvest emotional energy: Invest emotional energy in new people and goals.

Simon Rubin's Two Tracks of Bereavement

Simon Rubin is the director for the International Center for the Study of Loss, Bereavement, and Human Resilience at the University of Haifa in Israel. His two-track bereavement theory outlines an interactive process that is experienced within two realms. The first is an individual's bio-psycho-social functioning (including physical symptoms, anxiety, depression, relationships, and self-worth). The second realm is the grieving person's relationship with the person they lost (including emotional closeness, conflict, and preoccupation with their death). The two-track theory implies that to assess and cope with their grief, the grieving person needs to attend to both tracks of the process.

Stroebe and Schut's Dual Process Model of Grief

The dual process model of coping with grief was developed by Margaret Stroebe and Henk Schut, both professors and clinicians in the field of grief. They published the findings of their theory in a publication named "The Dual Process Model of Coping with Bereavement: A Decade On." In this publication, Stroebe and Schut theorized that grief operates according to two different processes and that people must oscillate, or switch back and forth, between these two processes as they grieve:

- **Loss-oriented:** In the loss-oriented grief process, the grieving individual experiences stressors that 1) make them think about their loved one and their death and 2) induce thoughts, feelings, actions, and events causing them to focus on their grief and pain. For instance, the grieving individual might look at photos of the person who has died and feel emotions like sadness, loneliness, and anger.

- **Restoration-oriented:** The restoration-oriented grief process is characterized by stressors that distract from grief and turn the grieving person's focus toward daily life and away from feelings of grief and pain. These stressors can include work, chores, exercise, and social activities. Stroebe and Schut believe that indulging in these distractions is a healthy way of coping with grief and that without this behavior, the grieving person would be unable to function in their day-to-day life.

- **Oscillation:** This term refers to the way that a grieving person moves back and forth between the two grief processes. According to Stroebe and Schut, the oscillation helps individuals emotionally work through and move forward after their loss.

Continuing Bonds Theory

The continuing bonds theory posits that the more linear models of grief end in a detachment from the person we've lost and therefore deny the reality of how most people grieve. The editors of the 1996 book *Continuing Bonds: New Understandings of Grief*, Dennis Klass, Phyllis R. Silverman, and Steven L. Nickman, suggested a new paradigm, rooted in the observation of healthy grief that does not resolve by detaching from the deceased but rather in creating a new relationship with the deceased.

In this model, grief isn't about working through a linear process that ends with acceptance or toward a new life where you have moved on or compartmentalized your loved one's memory. Rather, when a loved one dies, you slowly find ways to adjust and redefine your relationship with that person, allowing for a continued bond with that person that will continue, in different ways and to varying degrees, throughout your life. This relationship is not unhealthy, nor does it mean you are not grieving in a normal way. Instead, the continuing bonds theory suggests that keeping a relationship with a loved one who has passed is normal and healthy, and an important part of grief is continuing ties in this way.

Thomas Attig's Grief Process

Grief expert Thomas Attig's approach to grief is characterized by his suggestion that grieving is not a clinical problem to be solved or managed by others. In his process model, grieving is a normal process of relearning the world and our relationships with others in the aftermath of loss.

According to Attig, when we lose a loved one, we must adjust to a number of new variables to fully process our loss. We must adjust to changes in:

- Our physical world, including things like housing and the potential financial impact of the loss

- Our relationships with others who are still living, including the ways we relate to or depend on them

- Our perspectives on time, accommodating a new division between *before* our loss and *after* it

- Our spiritual grounding, including potentially dismissing or seeking belief systems that help us understand life and death

- Our relationship with the deceased, learning how to create a new relationship with them now that they are no longer physically here.

- Our identity, brought about by the experience of grieving and by the more practical changes that loss can bring to our lives

As mentioned, clients often find comfort in a model—any model—because it suggests certainty amid the confusing and sometimes chaotic expressions of grief. And if they have spent time considering their grief as a process, especially one that fits a model, they may think that deviations from this process are a cause for concern. For example, they may assume that there is only one acceptable way to grieve (and, typically, it is something closely resembling Kübler-Ross's five stages of grief). Because of this, clients might cling to one model, as it may seem to suit their current experience.

All of the previously discussed models offer different ways to approach a client's grieving process. One or more of the models may stand out to you. But it may be most useful to use different parts from many of the models to understand—and to help your clients understand—the different elements and presentations of the clients' experience of loss and grief.

CHALLENGES TO UNDERSTANDING GRIEF

Most clients will express some form of anxiety around their experience of grief, as they can bring on unexpected and frightening emotions, symptoms, behaviors, and even realizations. Grief work can be challenging this way, as one client's grief will not match another client's—and even separate grief journeys within the same person will likely differ as well.

The models of grief, though helpful, will never be able to account for every facet of someone's grief process—or the past grief they have already endured. Regardless of how closely your clients may hew to certain models, both clients and clinicians face challenges with identifying and understanding individual responses to loss and variations on the grief process. These challenges may be complicated by the variables described in this section.

HANDLING PREVIOUS OR MULTIPLE LOSSES

It's important to understand that a client's grieving process will change in the context of previous or multiple losses. Even if a client has already processed prior losses, these may impact their current grief. If, on the other hand, their history of loss includes *unprocessed* loss, they may experience cumulative grief.

It's inevitable that we will experience more than one loss in our lives. Sometimes it's the death of both parents. Sometimes it's a combination of family members and friends. Regardless of the circumstances, your clients may find that they are grappling with more than one loss at a time, whether because of a previous loss or two or more simultaneous ones. This can make clients feel confused and overwhelmed by the array of feelings that emerge while grieving losses together:

- Clients may feel overwhelmed by the amount of grief they are feeling.

- Clients may feel guilty that they are grieving one loss more than another.

- Clients may feel a heightened sense of anxiety.

- Clients may feel old grief reactivated by new grief.

- Clients may have trouble separating one loss from another.

Asking clients about their history of loss will provide clues about their current grief process. Such loss does not need to be specifically related to the death of a loved one, and clients may need your help to recognize other forms of grief, like pet loss, moving, or divorce, that have impacted (and continue to impact) them. Answers to the following questions can inform your approach to care.

 QUESTIONS FOR CLIENTS

Let's reflect on your experience with grief:

- Have you ever experienced grief and loss before now?
- How did those experiences shape your life?
- What did you learn about grief?
- What was helpful in those grief experiences?
- What do you wish you'd known then or done differently?
- How do those losses affect your current grief?

SEPARATING MULTIPLE LOSSES AND HONORING THEM

To manage the multiplication of grief, it is necessary for therapists and mental health professionals to tease apart all of a client's losses to look at them individually and then together as a whole.

Sometimes, if you do not provide enough support to your clients as they grieve multiple losses, they may feel that one or more of their losses are neglected. They may also feel as though they cannot access the grief associated with the losses that they now perceive, consciously or not, as disregarded. It's often easier to feel all the losses at once or to focus on one particular loss at a time. Therefore, finding ways to grieve the multiple losses together and to grieve the individual losses separately can be healing.

To support your clients as they honor their multiple losses, suggest that they set aside time to intentionally grieve their individual losses, especially if it seems that some losses are getting covered over by another loss. They can choose a day or a time that feels good and devote that time to grieving just one person. They can light candles, play music, look through old photos, or visit special and memorable places they went together.

You can also consider offering the following script:

> Take time to let yourself grieve for ALL that you have lost. Let yourself feel compassion for yourself that you have lost so much. Grieve for all the ways this has impacted your life and your feeling of safety in the world.

UNDERSTANDING THE RIPPLE EFFECT OF LOSS

It's useful to remember that no loss is a discrete or bounded event, especially in the case of previous and multiple losses. One client's loss connects to many other losses. And all of these losses must also be grieved. In fact, the wide range of loss impacts the wide range of emotions and feelings they experience when someone they love dies. This multidimensionality of loss is known as the *ripple effect of loss*. This radiating experience causes clients to not only consider the physical loss of their loved one but also:

- The loss of a shared life together and the things they did together
- The loss of a shared future, including hopes, dreams, and plans
- The loss of their shared social life
- The loss of the way their loved one(s) supported them physically, financially, and emotionally

REFLECTION

As you begin to understand a client's grieving process in the context of the major models of grief, as well as their history of loss, you can also encourage their reflection on their own experience of grieving. This may mean sharing details about major models of grief and inviting clients to consider the models, or parts of the models, that resonate with their own experience. This may also mean taking time in these early stages together to process and honor past or simultaneous losses that clients may newly grieve as a consequence of their current loss.

CHAPTER 4

NORMALIZING THE GRIEVING PROCESS

lthough the models in the previous chapter can help both you and your clients to approach and better understand the grieving process, these models can't fully capture your clients' emotions, feelings, behaviors, and physiological symptoms that occur in the wake of loss. Just as clients tend to feel anxiety about the right and wrong ways to grieve, they often feel anxiety about the specific emotions, feelings, behaviors, and physiological symptoms that manifest as they grieve.

I felt some of this in terms of my own grieving experience. When I was grieving my mom's death, I was consumed with guilt and fear. However, when I was grieving my dad's death, I was mostly sad and reflective. My point is, there are many ways to feel and experience grief, and they are all perfectly okay. As a therapists or mental health care professional, one of the most important tasks you fulfill as a companion to grief is to help clients see their grief as *normal* so as to accept, feel, and ultimately process and find peace with their experience of grief, no matter what it entails.

This chapter extends the conversation on understand grief as a whole. However, in this chapter, I integrate more targeted information, as well as more questions, to support clients in learning how to normalize and accept their own grieving process. This includes suggestions for helping clients to investigate their own preconceptions about grief and the blocks they might be experiencing in their grief. It also includes a discussion about the duration of grief and grief's long afterlife.

PREPARING TO NORMALIZE THE GRIEVING PROCESS

Many grieving clients experience confusion or anxiety about their grief. Although they are very familiar with the pain provoked by the loss of their person, they may feel upset or unsettled by the other emotions, feelings, behaviors, and physiological symptoms that seem to manifest alongside their grief. They may also feel upset by the places or times that their painful emotions, feelings, behaviors, or symptoms arise.

Therapists and mental health professionals can help normalize the experiences, expected and unexpected, that clients feel over the course of their grieving process. Normalization is key to acceptance, and acceptance is key to unblocking the grief that must be expressed so that it can be processed. To prepare for this work, you must reflect on your own preconceptions about grief.

For some readers, this may mean recalling a time before you experienced loss or before you began working with loss and grief. For others, it may mean remembering your grief and the ways that your grieving process may have surprised you.

QUESTIONS FOR THERAPISTS AND MENTAL HEALTH PROFESSIONALS

Reflect on your experiences with loss and grief:

- Have you ever been surprised by the ways that grief manifested?
- What expressions of grief have felt unexpected? What was it about these experiences that were surprising?

UNDERSTANDING PRECONCEPTIONS ABOUT GRIEF

Spending time educating clients about the different types of loss and grief and the different models of grief, as well as educating them on grief's presentations, enables them to approach their grief as a process, which begins the preparation of normalizing, and ultimately accepting, their experience.

Normalization is itself an active process. It begins when you provide your clients a broad education about grief and its major models. It extends beyond education when you guide your clients' attention to the particular ways grief has manifested, is manifesting, or might manifest in the future. You can encourage and structure your clients' reflections on their many and varied grief expressions to help them see and accept their grief as a normal process, even in its different expressions.

Normalization does not require fitting a client's experience into a preexisting model or pattern, but it's important to keep in mind that clients do not share your context of loss. You have likely seen grief present in an incredibly wide variety of emotions, feelings, expressions, behaviors, and symptoms. You may have even experienced some of these yourself. Your clients are on their own paths, however, and they only know about their own experience. Placing this experience on a spectrum isn't necessary, but establishing a wide spectrum of presentations of grief can help alleviate any anxiety they might feel, provide a sense of relief, and offer opportunities for identification.

When you approach the work of helping clients normalize their grieving process, begin the session with a few open-ended questions. Clients' answers will provide insight into their grieving process and will support your joint exploration of their concerns.

 QUESTIONS FOR CLIENTS

Let's consider the concept of grief:

- What did you think of grief before you experienced it?
- What have you observed about how others grieve?
- What do you think your grief should look/feel like?
- How long do you think your grief should last?
- What about your grief are you most afraid of?
- What do you think other people think about your grief?

WHAT TO EXPECT: NORMALIZING THE GRIEVING PROCESS

Although grief expressions often manifest in categorizable ways, these categories are not discrete or separable. Whereas some people may only feel sadness, sorrow, and anguish, others may feel a combination of disbelief and anguish and fear and rage. Still others may shift from resistance to guilt to anxiety to relief. As I'll continue to repeat, there is no right way to express grieve: All grief, even prolonged or complicated grief, is normal.

Your clients' answers to questions about their grief, as well as the story of loss they've shared with you, will inform what you prioritize when you discuss with them the following categories of grief expressions. Use the following section, *Expressions of Grief*, to provide psychoeducation to your clients on the different categories of grief. After conveying relevant selections, you can then use the questions after each expression to build connections between the information and the expressions of grief your clients are experiencing.

EXPRESSIONS OF GRIEF

Disbelief, Numbness, and Resistance

It is normal to feel some amount of resistance to loss. This is the brain's way of protecting us from the intensity of emotions that follow from loss. This is also why it is common to feel resistance in the first throes of grief.

After the loss of their person, clients may find themselves in a state of shock and disbelief. They may find themselves wanting to resist facing the reality of the situation. They may also feel numb and disconnected from reality, or they may feel as though they're disassociating. While disassociating, a person may feel as if they've shut down or are radically disconnected from themselves and from others.

 QUESTIONS FOR CLIENTS

Let's think about the role of numbness in your life:

- When have you felt numb or in shock?
- How long did this feeling last, and when did it change?
- Was there anything helpful about feeling this way?

Sadness, Sorrow, and Anguish

These are some of the most common feelings that accompany grief. But they are not always easy for everyone to feel. Some people may feel that if they let themselves open up to sorrow and sadness, they may never be able to stop crying. Others may have been taught by their culture or family that it is not okay to feel these tender emotions. Some people feel a general sense of sadness, and others may feel tormented by feelings of utter anguish.

QUESTIONS FOR CLIENTS

Let's consider the role of sadness in your life:

- When have you felt sad?
- Do you have difficulty or blocks to feeling sadness? Why, where, and when?
- Do you have any anxiety around sadness?

Anxiety and Fear

Feeling anxious and scared are very common feelings when clients are grieving. Their world has completely changed. Everything feels different now, and that's disorienting. They may feel afraid that they or someone else will die. They may feel afraid of getting sick. They may feel nervous about social situations. They may feel a general sense of unease or dread. They may have catastrophic thoughts and see disaster looming around every corner. They may experience panic attacks. These are *all* typical with grief. It is important to remind clients that anxiety is a normal—and sometimes useful—emotion, but there are ways to cope when it grows too big.

QUESTIONS FOR CLIENTS

Let's think about the role of anxiety in your life:

- When have you experienced anxiety in your life?
- What have you done to calm yourself in the past?
- When has anxiety been helpful?

Irritability, Anger, and Rage

Feelings of anger, irritability, and even rage are common responses in grief. Clients may experience anger over irrational things, or they may have very valid reasons to feel angry. They may find that they are angry at themselves, their deceased loved one, medical professionals, family members and friends, and even strangers. Anger is a powerful emotion that usually serves to cover up more vulnerable emotions such as sadness and fear. For this reason, clients may struggle to feel anger at all, even if others expect them to be angry.

QUESTIONS FOR CLIENTS

Let's think about the role of anger in your life:

- What are your associations with anger?
- Do you have difficulty or blocks to feeling anger? Why, where, and when?
- What's underneath your anger?

Guilt and Regret

Feelings of guilt and regret are common companions to grief. When clients lose someone they love, it's difficult not to imagine what could have been different. Sometimes they regret choices they made in regard to caregiving. Sometimes they had unresolved issues with the person they lost. It is typical for clients to feel guilty or regret their actions as part of the grieving process, but there are tools and methods for helping them move through these emotions.

 QUESTIONS FOR CLIENTS

Let's think about guilt and regret in relation to your loss:

- Is there anything you regret or feel guilty about in regard to the person you lost?
- What do guilt and regret feel like in your body?
- What would it be like to let go of guilt and regret?

Hope and Relief

Sometimes clients will feel relief with the death of a loved one, and this can be a confusing feeling. Remind them that it's okay to feel relief, joy, pleasure, and even hopeful about the future. Feeling those things doesn't mean they are not grieving—it means they are a human experiencing a wide range of emotions. At the same time, if they don't feel these things right now, let them know that that's okay too.

 QUESTIONS FOR CLIENTS

Let's consider the feelings of hope and relief within your current experience:

- Are there any ways you feel relieved by your loved one's death?
- Are there times when you are experiencing joy and pleasure in your life, even while you are grieving?
- Do you feel hopeful about the future even though you are grieving?

NORMALIZING GRIEF'S DURATION

Why do some people grieve for short periods of time and others for longer? There are many different factors that affect the length of time each person will experience grief, and the research about the length of time people grieve is ever-expanding. One of the most common trajectories for grief is the *one-year arc*, which is characterized by a year of firsts. I also discuss what author and grief expert Hope Edelman calls "the aftergrief," which refers to the experiences of grief the extend well beyond the first year.

Some clients take a long time to process experiences and emotions, and others move through them more quickly. If a client is comfortable feeling and expressing emotions, they may have an easier time being in their grief, and therefore, moving through it. But some clients tend to struggle to access emotions, and their grief may take longer to process. On the flipside, if clients feel things deeply, they may find that they feel them for longer.

Other factors, such as family and community support, health, secondary losses, life obligations and circumstances, and religious or spiritual beliefs, can also impact the length of time clients grieve. Prior trauma, older losses, and other hardships in life may prolong or reactivate grief.

To support your clients in approaching their sense of grief's duration, guide them both in and outside of session to answer the following questions:

 QUESTIONS FOR CLIENTS

Let's reflect on the duration of grief:

- How long do you think grief lasts?
- Where do you think these ideas came from?
- What do you want your own grief process to look like?
- Where you want to be in a year?
- What are your biggest blocks or fears around grief?

VISUALIZING THE TIMELINE OF GRIEF

As with the wide spectrum of grief, there is no right amount of time to spend in the grieving process. Clients process their grief in different ways and according to different timelines. Consider the following visuals depicting the process of grief's duration, and consider sharing the figures with your clients to give them a variety of models to visualize their own grief process.

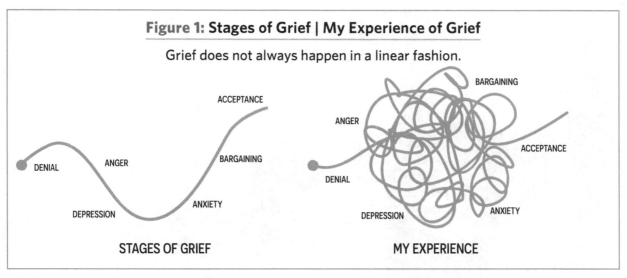

Figure 1: Stages of Grief | My Experience of Grief

Grief does not always happen in a linear fashion.

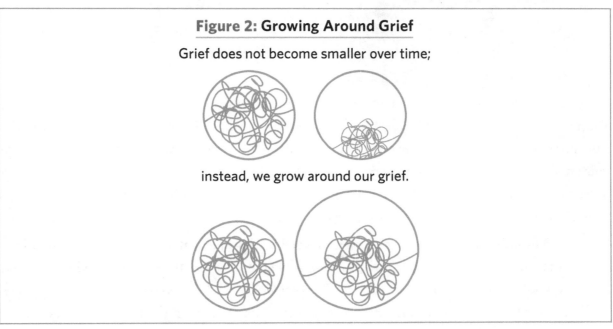

Figure 2: Growing Around Grief

Grief does not become smaller over time;

instead, we grow around our grief.

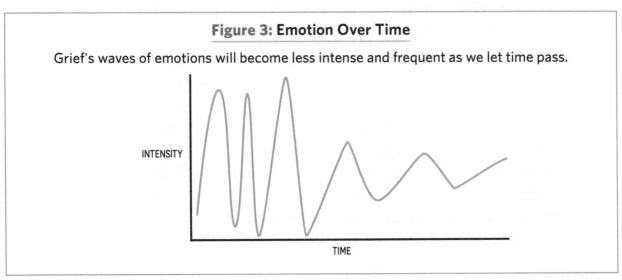

Figure 3: Emotion Over Time

Grief's waves of emotions will become less intense and frequent as we let time pass.

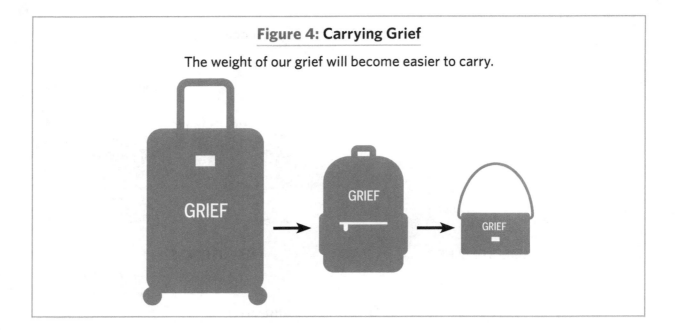

Figure 4: Carrying Grief

The weight of our grief will become easier to carry.

CONSIDERING THE ONE-YEAR ARC

Over my years of grief work, I have observed an arc of emotions and feelings that commonly occur within the first year of loss. This timeline isn't the same for each person—and of course, any emotion can appear at any stage—but more often than not, clients' experiences correlate to it. It offers a useful context for establishing a client's course of care. It can be helpful to introduce the one-year arc as a very general timeline for grief. It can be an especially useful tool when helping to normalize the changes that may occur for clients during their first year of grief.

- **0–3 months:** This period is often characterized by shock, denial, anxiety, and confusion. In these first months it can be difficult—impossible for some—to fully comprehend the loss and to understand the scope of its impact. This period can also be filled with practical obligations, such as funeral planning and estate management, family negotiations, financial distress, and other responsibilities, which can preoccupy the griever to the point that they do not have the bandwidth to let themselves feel some emotions, even if they may need to.

- **3–6 months:** It is typically during this time period when the initial feelings of grief are truly felt. Sadness, despair, anger, and anxiety often surface in significant ways. While this can be the most difficult period of grief for the person who has experienced loss, it can appear to be a contradictory manifestation of grief given the cultural expectations around the griever. Three to six months after a loss, community support has often dropped off. The griever is typically expected to be getting back to their regular life. The difference between the griever's experience and the community's expectations can cause distress and anxiety, and it is often during this time period that clients seek therapy and other forms of support.

- **6–9 months:** Although each period is difficult in its own way, this period is a heavy one. The reality of the loss, though not necessarily the acceptance of it, has typically set in for the griever, and they may be struggling to adjust to the world without their loved one. Additionally, at this point, the grieving person will have been through a series of firsts, including first holidays and anniversaries without their loved one, and the first time something good or bad happens in their life without their loved one to share in it. This period can also mark the longest someone has gone without their loved one in their life. Of course, as with the three- to six-month period, at this point, most grievers are expected—by society's expectations—to have moved through the hardest parts of their grief. This can be especially painful for grievers because they may be feeling their loss more than ever.

- **9–12 months:** This period leads up to the one-year anniversary of the death of the loved one and can fill a grieving person with a sense of anticipation, anxiety, and dread. As they approach the one-year mark, the griever may have the experience of reliving the weeks or months leading up to their loved one's death. This period also marks the end of the first holidays and anniversaries without their loved one. Making plans for the one-year anniversary, whether a person chooses to honor their loved one in a particular way or do nothing at all, is an important part of easing the anxiety that accompanies the buildup to this date.

ANTICIPATING THE YEAR OF FIRSTS

The initial year after a loved one's death is marked by firsts and other important signs of passing time. Some of these are as simple as a first trip to the grocery store after a loved one's death, and some are bigger, such as celebrating a birthday without your person for the first time. As a practitioner, you can anticipate some of these markers and help your clients navigate the anxiety and uncertainty that comes with facing them. Although some experiences will come as a surprise, some will be dates and occasions that you and your clients can plan for. The following list offers a few examples that clients may find helpful to discuss:

- The first time you must unexpectedly tell someone, such as a doctor or store clerk with whom you've had a friendly relationship, that your loved one is gone

- The first time you go to an event, such as a party or a concert, without your loved one

- The first time you travel without your loved one

- The first time you visit a shared favorite place without them

- The first time you go back to work

- The first time you surpass the longest you've gone without seeing or talking to your loved one

- The first time you want to tell your loved one about something good that has happened

- The first time you want to tell them about something hard that has happened

- The beginning of a new season without them

- Their birthday, your birthday, or other loved ones' birthdays
- The first holidays without them

Clients might find none, some, or all of these firsts to be incredibly painful. Sometimes, the pain or hurt is unexpected. For example, someone may expect to feel bad when something bad happens to them, but they may not realize that this pain can be significantly compounded when they realize they can't share the news with their loved one. Even good things can cause pain when clients are unable to share their happiness with the person they've lost.

Meanwhile, obvious passages of time, such as the changing of the seasons, can serve as a reminder that life is moving forward despite a loved one's absence. The holidays can pose particular challenges because they're often considered to be part of a cheerful and joyous season. Feeling unable to partake in this cheer can contribute to feelings of isolation, adding loneliness to our grief. Birthdays, including the grieving person's own birthday, may be difficult for similar reasons, as they are often a painful reminder of the hole that was once filled by a loved one's presence.

During this year of firsts, it is important to acknowledge with clients the many potential challenges that stand in their path as a grieving person. In your role as a companion to grief, you can offer them support by providing this acknowledgment and by encouraging the griever to decide ahead of time how they want to commemorate various occasions.

It is also important to support people as they communicate their needs around commemoration to family members and friends. Helping clients to decide in advance how they want to spend some of their first experiences without their loved one and how to gain the support of family and friends can decrease the anxiety that comes with the anticipation.

To support your clients as they prepare for their own year of firsts, ask them to respond to the prompts in the following questions, which serves two purposes: They solicit the clients' reflection on important topics relevant to their grief, and they also help to normalize aspects of the grieving process that clients might not expect. The responses to the prompts offer a client-centered way to approach some of these unanticipated or unwelcome parts of the grieving process. Discuss their responses with them, and then help to identify potential opportunities for easing their fears.

(?) QUESTIONS FOR CLIENTS

Let's consider what your year of firsts will bring:

- Consider any *first* occasions that might be helpful for you to anticipate.
- For each occasion, answer the following:
  - How do you imagine you will feel on the day?
  - How can you plan to cope with the day?
  - How might you honor your person on the day?
  - How can you ask friends/family to support you on the day?

CHALLENGES TO NORMALIZING THE GRIEVING PROCESS

Clients are frequently surprised when they realize that their grieving process will not end, at least not in a conventional way, after a year or two. While they will process their loss and find closure, they will likely continue to experience grief for the rest of their lives. This can be a painful realization. In fact, some clients may even panic when they learn that their grief will be a lasting part of their lives. This pain and panic are often due to the assumption that their most overwhelming and intense experiences of grief will endure in later years. But this is not typically the case.

It's important to help your clients understand that they will not always feel the intensity associated with early grief, nor will they always feel the anguish that often characterizes unprocessed grief. They will process their loss and find closure, but they will continue to grieve in the years to come. To help clients understand and accept this, normalize the changing shape of grief by talking about what grief may look like in the future.

PREPARING FOR THE AFTERGRIEF

The aftergrief period can present a wide variety of challenges. The loss a client sustains when their loved one dies never goes away, and yet, they have only just begun to recognize all the ways this loss can play out in their lifetime. Losses can impact the ability to be in a relationship, parenting choices, lifestyle decisions, career paths, issues with substance abuse and addiction, and even overall health.

I have worked with many clients who have experienced a loss five years, ten years, and even two or three decades ago and who want or need to process how the loss has impacted their choices, their direction in life, and their functioning. Edelman defines this process as "the aftergrief." The aftergrief helps to name and describe the long arc of loss and its effect on our lives, and Edelman offers important insights into the ways that old grief can be triggered anew, especially by events like childbirth, divorce, and aging.

This should not be taken to mean that someone will be beholden to their grief for the rest of their life. But it does mean that clients in this period of their grieving process may have particular needs. One of the needs may simply be the normalization of the long impact of loss.

It's also important to acknowledge that the aftergrief period is also defined and characterized by the ways loss helps to make meaning in your clients' lives, shapes their positive experiences, and helps them to refine their sense of identity and fulfillment in life. While loss is painful, it can also provoke meaning-making and growth.

UNDERSTANDING THE AFTERGRIEF OF OLDER LOSSES

In her book *The Aftergrief,* Edelman describes the different kinds of grief we experience as the years move forward as well as the ways our grief changes. According to Edelman, the arc of grief moves from "new grief" to "old grief." However, old grief will not necessarily stay in the past—it is characterized by cyclical grief, grief sneak attacks, and resurrected grief, among others. The information that follows is based on this important work.

New Grief (Here and Now)

New grief is the raw, immediate grief that comes with an initial loss. It is a physical and emotional experience and a feeling that didn't exist before. The emotions are a combination of panic, anguish, sorrow, anxiety, anger, relief, guilt, and hopelessness, among others. This new grief often feels unbearable and impossible to withstand. Your clients' innate coping skills of avoidance and denial may surface during this time as a way to give them breaks from this kind of acute grief.

New grief is something that clients can feel multiple times as they experience subsequent losses throughout their lives. Each experience of new grief remains specific and unique to the person your client has lost, defined by their relationship, how their person died, and their current life circumstances and level of support. It doesn't necessarily become easier, but it does become more familiar.

When your clients experience new grief, they may feel that it will never end, but they should understand that new grief will eventually give way to old grief.

Old Grief (Recurrent and Resurgent)

While new grief is a present-day reaction to a recent loss, Edelman defines old grief as "a response in the present to a loss from the past." Old grief is recurrent and unpredictable and sometimes difficult to decipher. When old grief suddenly surfaces for clients, especially those who feel they have been on steady ground for a while, they may feel shaken or even ashamed for thinking that they had been doing okay when now they clearly aren't.

Old grief surfaces when a trigger in the present reactivates the thoughts and emotions connected to a client's loss. These resurgences of old grief are typically temporary and short-lived, but they should expect flare-ups throughout their lives. The following sections are forms of old grief.

Cyclical Grief

An aspect of old grief, cyclical grief often resurges around dates of remembrance, such as a loved one's birthday, Mother's Day, or the anniversary of a death. However, cyclical grief can also be evoked by a time of day, a day of the week, or a season. If, for instance, a client's person died on a Tuesday, or in the spring, they may feel cyclical grief on that day of the week or the start of that season.

Cyclical grief is often expressed through somatic reactions, meaning clients may feel this grief in their bodies before they are conscious of it or its source. Clients may feel "off," disoriented, sad, or irritable in the days leading up to a particularly potent date or time without knowing why. When they are conscious of an impending date looming, they may feel anxiety leading up to the day—this anxiety is often worse than the experience of the day itself.

With each recurring date, cumulative grief can build, and a client can feel bowed under the weight of yet another birthday missed, another Mother's Day without a mom, or another holiday gathering in the absence of a loved one. As the years go by, grieving individuals generally find themselves alone in observing these dates. The support they once received has almost certainly ebbed. Finding ways to help clients anticipate these dates, identify support and put it in place, and find ways to honor their grief can offer immense relief.

Grief Sneak Attacks

Grief sneak attacks occur when old grief is unexpectedly triggered, often by a sense experience. Something like a song on the radio, a smell associated with a loved one, or even crossing paths with someone who looks like the person who died can provoke a grief sneak attack. These kinds of triggers are impossible to anticipate and can instantly evoke acute feelings of sadness and longing.

Resurrected grief

Resurrected grief occurs when a new loss in the present—a phase of *new* grief—reactivates old grief from a loss from the past. This affects clients even more when old grief has been suppressed or trauma has not been processed. Resurrected grief can also occur when clients go through a major life change, such as a big move, career shift, breakup, or divorce. When grief is resurrected in these instances, they find themselves grieving the past, the present, and the past *within* the present.

New Old Grief (One-Time Transitions)

New old grief refers to the present experience of a grief from a past loss. It is a new iteration of an old grief, and it often manifests around one-time transitions that clients value in relationship to their loved one who has passed. After a loss, they may contemplate what it will feel like to move through future life events without their person, but they cannot truly know the grief these events will trigger until they are in these moments, experiencing those events. For instance, even though someone has acknowledged their parent will not be able to see them get married, the grief they feel when they actually walk down the aisle is something new within the old grief.

Clients will experience new old grief as they mature and cross thresholds from one life phase into another, finding themselves yearning anew for someone they lost as they experience an aspect of life they wish they were here for. Even during some of their happiest moments, they may feel waves of sadness and grief that their person is not here to celebrate with them.

New old grief often surfaces during age-related dates. Clients may feel new old grief when turning the age their person was when they died. Or they may feel new old grief when they reach a death anniversary that marks the time when their person has been gone longer than they were alive. They may experience new old grief when their child reaches the same age that the client was when they experienced their loss. These dates can become quite significant in clients' lives—often creating anxiety or serving as motivation for life goals—but they almost always evoke this new old grief.

Clients in the aftergrief period may require a different approach than clients whose loss is more recent. For instance, clients with an older loss may want to reflect not only on the loss itself but on their prior experience of grief and the impact of their grieving process on their life choices. To surface some of these concerns, guide the client through a comprehensive discussion of the aftergrief period in session.

 QUESTIONS FOR CLIENTS

Let's reflect on your aftergrief period:

- What was your grief like in the early years of the loss?
- What were the messages you received about grief?
- Do you feel you were able to fully grieve at the time of loss?
- How has the loss shaped your life throughout the years?
- At what points has the loss and grief resurfaced for you?
- How do you feel the loss has impacted your relationships?
- How has the loss affected your anxiety?

REFLECTION

Often, grieving clients' discomfort or anxiety around their experience of grief drives their decision to seek therapeutic support. As a therapists and mental health professional, you can provide education, but you can also work with grieving clients to normalize their specific experiences. Normalization does not result in alleviation of pain, but it can offer release and comfort. When you meet your clients where they are, whether in the throes of early grief or in a period of reflection after many years, you offer acceptance and normalization in a therapeutic environment. Often, the services you render strengthens your clients' resilience and enables them to continue processing their grief, whenever and however it arises.

CHAPTER 5

RESPONDING TO GRIEF ANXIETY

No one ever told me that grief felt so like fear.

—C.S. Lewis

experienced my first panic attack when I was eighteen years old. My high school boyfriend and I were on a road trip, visiting each other's new college campuses. The trip was exciting, and I felt hopeful for the future. At the same time, I knew that my sick parents weren't getting better and that I'd soon be far from them, traveling a different path.

As my boyfriend and I drove home, my mood shifted from hopeful to helpless and back again. Suddenly, the unbearable weight of all the things I couldn't control slammed into my chest. I felt a crushing sensation in my heart and lungs, and as I began to gasp for air, my vision tunneled, and I became dizzy. Out of what felt like nowhere, I couldn't breathe. I couldn't see straight. I couldn't even talk. I had no clue what was happening to me. My boyfriend drove me to the nearest emergency room, but I was diagnosed with heart palpitations and nothing more.

At the time, I didn't connect my physical symptoms with anxiety. I certainly didn't connect my anxiety with the grief I felt over my parents' sicknesses or my fear over their deaths. Instead, I spent the next years confused by and afraid of the episodes that occurred more and more frequently, especially after the death of my mother. It wasn't until I started down my own path toward healing that I realized I was experiencing grief anxiety.

Many clients who struggle with grief anxiety feel similarly bewildered. Although the death of their person may have taken them by surprise, they usually expect to feel the sadness, pain, and hurt associated with grief. They do not always expect to also feel the fear and dread of anxiety, nor do they expect anxiety to manifest in physical symptoms that are difficult to predict and hard to control.

From a clinical perspective, the connection between anxiety and grief should not be surprising: Anxiety often accompanies loss, particularly a loss that upends your clients' lives, reminds them of their inability to control the future, and underscores their human vulnerability. Yet, clients and clinicians alike are only just beginning to understand the many ways that anxiety and grief are connected.

Clients in grief experience anxiety in a variety of ways and for a variety of reasons. Some clients may have never experienced anxiety before the loss of their person and are confused and upset by their symptoms; others may have had a lifelong relationship with anxiety but do not recognize the forms it takes after their loss. Clients may have experienced some aspects of anxiety prior to the loss of their person but experience different or more intense aspects of anxiety afterward.

Whether clients are just beginning to connect their anxiety with their grief or are more in tune to the correlation, they will benefit from therapeutic support. Therapists and mental health care professionals can help to normalize clients' experience of grief anxiety, provide education about their experience of grief anxiety, and explain tips and tools that can help them manage their experiences.

Providing support to anxiously grieving clients requires a tandem approach. You must listen to clients' experiences of grief anxiety while also helping to normalize their grief *and* their anxiety up front. You must also recognize that clients will often seek aid after a panic attack or other emergent anxiety symptoms, meaning they likely want or need immediate relief.

In this chapter, I discuss how to prepare to work with clients experiencing grief anxiety; what to expect with clients experiencing grief anxiety; the potential causes, types, and manifestations of grief anxiety; the process that therapists and mental health professionals can use to normalize grief anxiety; and the most accessible tools for responding to clients with grief anxiety. I also include a number of questions, prompts, and activities that can be used during sessions to help clients find immediate relief.

My hope is to normalize grief anxiety not only for clients but for therapists and mental health professionals too, so that those who experience loss do not also feel the confusion and pain that I felt before I learned more about my own grief anxiety.

PREPARING TO RESPOND TO GRIEF ANXIETY

Clients with grief anxiety may or may not know that they are experiencing grief anxiety. They may or may not be activated during sessions. They may or may not be responsive to education or to tips and tools associated with managing their symptoms. As a therapist or mental health professionals, you already know you can control at least one factor: your own preparation. To ready yourself to work with anxiously grieving clients, you can first review and reflect on the role—positive *and* negative— that anxiety plays in your own life.

QUESTIONS FOR THERAPISTS AND MENTAL HEALTH PROFESSIONALS

Take a few moments to think about the role anxiety has played in your own life:

- When has anxiety been helpful for you?
- When has it been harmful?
- Do you use any strategies to retain its helpfulness while reducing its harmfulness?

CAUSES OF GRIEF ANXIETY

Although anxiety can appear in different forms and at any point in the grieving process, persistent grief anxiety often results from one or more relatively predictable causes. Typically, these causes are unified by their association with ongoing efforts to suppress, fend off, or find protection from the incredibly strong emotions that accompany loss.

Suppressive efforts frequently take the following forms, which often provoke or otherwise relate to a variety of anxiety symptoms.

Blocked Grief

This is a form of incomplete mourning and is often expressed through avoidance-based behaviors. Clients experiencing blocked grief may strenuously avoid topics of conversation, or they may report avoiding people, places, things, and activities that remind them of the person they've lost. They may also repeatedly downplay or minimize their loss, suggesting that their experience is "no big deal."

Alternatively, clients experiencing blocked grief may express fixation behaviors. For instance, clients may excessively revisit certain topics of conversation that remind them of their person. They may report enshrining objects associated with their person or engaging in ritualistic activities that appear to venerate their person.

While behaviors associated with avoidance and fixation are very common in grief, clients struggling with grief anxiety often express these behaviors in excessive or disruptive ways. The work of pushing away all reminders of their person, of downplaying their experience of pain, or of vigilantly keeping their person at the forefront of their mind can arrest the grieving process. Symptoms of anxiety may then manifest as a proxy for the strong emotions associated with grief.

Guilt

Many clients grieving the loss of a loved one experience guilt. Clients feel guilty for a variety of reasons, rational and seemingly irrational. They may feel guilty because they did not predict or were not able to prevent their person's death. They may feel some form of survivor's guilt. They may feel guilt associated with their prior relationship with their person or with words that were said or left unsaid. They may also feel guilt associated with their own grief response.

When guilt manifests, it is often related to the impression of a lack of control after the death of a loved one, especially in consideration with grief and the grieving process. Guilt can develop into grief anxiety when clients stay stuck in their feelings of guilt, unable to move on or to experience closure.

Anger

Anger is a primary emotion in grief and constitutes one of the stages in Elisabeth Kübler-Ross's five-stage grief model. As I discussed in the previous chapter, clients can experience grief-associated anger as irritability, indignation, rage, or resentment. They might be angry at their loved one who has died, at medical professionals, at family members, at friends, at strangers, at god, at the universe, at themselves, and at us, their companion in grief.

For many clients, anger can be easier or more familiar to feel than the consuming pain associated with their loss. These clients may hold onto a shield of anger to deflect the sharper, less familiar feelings provoked by death like fear, anguish, and uncertainty. However, because anger is an insufficient protector, clients who hold too tightly to their anger and for too long may also experience symptoms of grief anxiety. Anger can be a powerful emotion, and it is often difficult for clients to move through their anger. Chapter 10 describes more specific strategies for supporting clients as they process their anger.

Traumatic Death of Loved One

Often, a traumatic death is unexpected or occurs outside the bounds, sometimes very far outside the bounds, of more typical experiences of life and death. When a loved one's death is traumatic, clients may feel as though the fabric of the universe has been torn, exposing previously unseen chaos.

Clients might also have experienced trauma associated with witnessing or surviving their loved one's death. They may feel profoundly alone, detached from their previous life and relationships, and unable to express themselves or to speak about or otherwise assimilate the newfound and unwanted knowledge of their trauma. In this way, the traumatic death of a loved one may result in the suppression of strong emotions that then manifest as grief anxiety.

Prolonged Illness or Death of Loved One

Prolonged illness or death may suggest the possibility of preparation, but preparedness does not typically decrease the pain of grief. In fact, during their loved one's prolonged illness, clients often radically narrow their focus for extended periods of time onto their loved one's daily survival. When death occurs, these clients must quickly widen their focus to include the many parts of their life that were "on hold" while they attended to their loved one.

This new and necessary broader focus can be overwhelming, especially because it frequently includes urgent administrative and organizational duties associated with a loved one's death. Clients may experience symptoms of grief anxiety, in part, as a result of the disorientation and overwhelm.

Family Dynamics

When a loved one dies, family systems change, and family dynamics often reorganize in new and unpredictable ways. Clients may subsequently find that after the death of their loved one, their primary support system has fundamentally altered. They may experience new frictions with family members, or they may experience unfamiliar dynamics within what were once intimately understood relationships. Additionally, grief is experienced differently by different people. These differences can test family relationships, affecting the support sought and provided in the short and long term.

The importance of family systems and the inability to control the inevitable shifts in family dynamics after the death of a loved one can be a significant source of stress in client grief, increasing clients' discomfort in ways that make closure difficult and grief anxiety common. See chapter 6 for a further discussion of approaching family dynamics through the lens of grief.

Fear of Death

When a loved one dies, clients must confront, in one way or another, the primal fear of their own death. For anxiously grieving clients, their fears over their own death and over the potential deaths of their family members and friends are often at the forefront of their minds. When these fears are persistent, excessive, and disruptive, they can paralyze some clients, rendering them unable to undertake action that could soothe their fears and associated anxiety.

As with guilt and anger, the fear of death can function for some clients as a painful substitute for the even more uncomfortable emotions associated with grief. Suppressing those emotions can provoke symptoms of grief anxiety.

Overwhelming Life Changes

The death of a loved one changes everything, from day-to-day activities to relationships with family members and friends. For some clients, the death of their person can also require substantial changes in a living situation, professional status, health insurance, financial stability, and other core areas of life. Some clients may have to quickly move, find a new job, procure new health insurance, or figure out ways to stabilize their finances.

Just one of these changes can be hard for clients to handle, but together in one time frame, and for people who are also grieving, they can result in overwhelm and paralysis. It is not unusual for clients who are facing significant change to their living situation to experience symptoms of grief anxiety in response to this kind of overwhelm.

WHAT TO EXPECT: RESPONDING TO GRIEF ANXIETY

Those dealing with grief anxiety are often inhabiting an unknown, unexplored land. As mentioned earlier, clients may be experiencing grief for the first time. They may be experiencing anxiety or certain symptoms of anxiety for the first time, especially in the context of grief. Therapists and mental health professionals must therefore take the lead, screening clients for grief anxiety and supporting them as they make connections between their grief and their anxiety.

Anxiety often indicates that emotions or feelings associated with grief have been suppressed or repressed, closing both the course of grief and the path for healing. Therefore, clinicians should be aware of the common expressions or challenges of anxiety that may cause clients to have difficulty expressing, manifesting, or working through their grief.

By identifying our anxiously grieving clients and offering them support, you act as a guide through uncharted territory and help them find their way. Clients suffering from grief-related anxiety often present with the expressions and challenges found in the next section.

COMMON EXPRESSIONS OF GRIEF ANXIETY

Expressions of anxiety related to the grieving process are not always unlike expressions of other types of anxiety. Though helping your clients to cope with their anxiety symptoms will not eliminate their grief all together, relieving their anxiety will help to move them through the course of grief and toward healing. The following are some of the most common expressions of grief anxiety:

- **Agitation and restlessness:** Clients experiencing grief anxiety may be agitated and restless. They may struggle to sit still or to remain seated. They may prefer to pace or walk around the room. Some clients may rock back and forth as a self-soothing strategy, or they may demonstrate excessive fidgeting behaviors, such as bouncing their legs up and down, restlessly picking up and putting down items, or continuously opening up and rearranging the items in their pockets or bags. Agitated or restless clients may find relief through supported exercises that foster regulation, such as deep, diaphragmatic breathing exercises. They may find it useful to synchronize their breathing by counting aloud or watching glitter or snow settle in a snow globe or similar object. If possible, these clients may also find comfort in walking sessions.

- **Anxiety about anxiety:** Some clients may experience anxiety even from talking about anxiety. For these clients, focusing their attention on their anxiety can cause unacknowledged, unknown, or overlooked symptoms associated with anxiety to rush in. For other clients, focusing on their anxiety may provoke fears about feeling more anxious, which in turn provokes further or more intense anxiety. You can support these clients by helping them to slow down, limiting their focus to just one anxiety symptom and its connections to grief, and taking frequent breaks to check in and practice diaphragmatic breathing.

- **Difficulty talking about grief:** Many clients find it challenging to discuss their grief, but clients who are reluctant to reference their grief or who face inordinate struggle when trying to communicate their grief may be experiencing anxiety, especially as it relates to feelings of fear and overwhelm. These clients may benefit from questions that encourage a curious approach to their grieving experiences or those that help them identify the support they believe they need.

- **Difficulty talking about anxiety:** Sometimes, clients are so immersed in their grief that they are not able to recognize or to communicate about their other experiences, especially anxiety-related experiences. These clients may benefit from questions that enable them to make connections between their feelings of grief and their physical sensations. For instance, when clients discuss the pain of their loss, ask questions that help them locate what they feel in their body when they talk about their loss: a constricted throat, a wavering or tremulous voice, a tensing of shoulders, an increased heart rate? You can then help clients to build further connections to the potential cognitive and behavioral symptoms of anxiety that may be related to their grief.

- **Preference for anxiety over grief:** For some clients, their symptoms of anxiety may feel safer, more familiar, or easier to discuss than feelings associated with grief. It may be useful to help support these clients as they identify and make connections between the physical manifestations of anxiety and their deeper, unattended grief. Explaining the link between a recognized physical symptom, such as an increased heart rate, shortness of breath, dizziness, sweating, or nausea, and their feelings of fear, anger, and overwhelm can open the door to broader discussion about the ways that fear, anger, and overwhelm relate to the grieving process.

IDENTIFYING BLOCKS TO GRIEVING

After introducing clients to grief anxiety and its applicable expressions, open a wide-ranging discussion with clients about their own grief anxiety. Some clients may not have considered their anxiety through the lens of grief—or their grief through the lens of anxiety. Consequently, you can use the following questions for client education.

 QUESTIONS FOR CLIENTS

Let's think about the relationship between your grief and your anxiety:

- Do you feel you have fully grieved?
- Take a moment and target the specific areas that you feel you need to work on.
- Do you feel you have experienced one grief emotion more than another? For example, have you felt predominately numb, or have you been mostly steeped in depression?
- Is there something blocking you from moving through your grief? Perhaps a stigma around experiencing emotions? Or a sense of guilt about something involving your loved one?
- Do you feel you need additional support in order to express your grief? If so, what or from whom would that look like?

COMMON TYPES OF GRIEF ANXIETY

Grief can change or worsen the symptoms commonly associated with different types of anxiety. Clients experiencing specific types of anxiety may experience symptoms in ways that are intrinsically connected to the loss of their person and the subsequent pain of grief. The following are the most common types of grief anxiety:

- **Generalized anxiety:** Clients experiencing generalized anxiety after the death of their loved one may feel constant worry or a pervasive sense of dread. This is often associated with fear, particularly a fear of the unknown that is provoked by an inability to control the future. Clients experiencing generalized anxiety while grieving may feel restless or have trouble sleeping, in part because they are preoccupied with grief-related feelings of fear, guilt, or anger. For these clients, the constant worry that often characterizes generalized anxiety may feel warranted or rational, particularly in relationship to the death of their loved one.

- **Panic attacks:** Grieving clients experiencing panic attacks may experience these attacks in relationship to a sense of impending doom or terror related to the death of their loved one, or they may be related to the fear of their own death or the deaths of others. Clients may experience panic attacks when thinking about the future or when discussing the overwhelming life changes that they must make as a consequence of the loss of their person. Clients may also experience a cascade of feelings of grief, or they may *fear* a cascade of feelings of grief—including fear, anger, helplessness, and vulnerability—resulting in a racing heart, lightheadedness, tingling sensations, shaking, nausea, or hyperventilating.

- **Hypochondria:** Grief anxiety hypochondria may manifest as a preoccupation with getting sick or seriously ill, or it may manifest as attributing minor bodily symptoms to serious illness. It is frequently associated with the fear of the unknown, specifically the fear of death that can follow the loss of a loved one. Clients with grief anxiety manifesting as hypochondria may become easily alarmed about their health status, finding no reassurance from doctors or negative test results. They may fixate on their health, practicing constant vigilance in an effort to be better prepared for future sickness or injury.

- **Obsessive compulsive behavior:** Clients with grief anxiety may experience obsessive compulsive behaviors in the form of intrusive, obsessive thoughts about their loved one or about feelings associated with the loss of their loved one, including feelings of fear and anger. This is a common manifestation of anxiety, fear, and worry and can in some cases be triggered by grief anxiety. Alternatively, obsessive compulsive behaviors may function as a response to the many challenges associated with the acute fear and uncertainty that can follow the death of a loved one. Such behaviors may or may not have to do with fears of contamination or dirt, the need for things to be orderly and symmetrical, and an intolerance of uncertainty. Some clients, these behaviors may manifest as excessively repetitive or ritualistic behaviors about or related to the person who has died.

- **Posttraumatic stress disorder (PTSD):** While some clients witness the traumatic death of their loved one, other clients may experience their bereavement itself as a personal trauma. Clients can experience elements of PTSD related to their loved one's death, including nightmares or unwanted memories of the trauma, avoidance of situations that bring back memories of the trauma, anxiety, depressed moods, and heightened reactions to stimuli or, alternatively, numbness. Generally, clients with grief anxiety that manifests as PTSD may also struggle to accept their loss, may engage in a variety of avoidance behaviors around the topic of their loss, and may detach or not trust others because of the trauma surrounding their loss.

- **Social phobias:** Phobias can arise or be exacerbated by the death of a loved one. Sometimes, clients feel isolated and alone in their grief, or they may feel unable to function in the presence of others who do not know about or share their grief (or even those who *are* aware of their grief). Clients with grief anxiety that manifests in social phobias may feel that their grief or the death of their loved one has made them conspicuously abnormal. They may describe excess fear of situations where they feel they may be judged, or they may worry about embarrassment or humiliation. They may also feel concern about offending someone. They may also want to avoid all social situations because they associate social situations with feeling vulnerable and out of control.

- **Specific phobias:** Clients with grief anxiety that manifests in specific phobias feel excessive or irrational fears of a specific object or situation, avoiding the object or situation or only tolerating it under extreme duress. As with many other types and manifestations of grief anxiety, clients with grief expressed through specific phobias may be suppressing powerful emotions and feelings associated with grief, and they may be focusing instead, though not purposefully, on fears that seem to be more easily avoided or managed.

- **Separation anxiety:** When clients experience grief anxiety as separation anxiety, it can be related to the radical separation they experienced after the death of their loved one. This manifests as recurrent and excessive distress about anticipating being away or actually being away from loved ones who are still living; constant and excessive worry about losing a loved one; and avoidance of situations that cause or may be perceived to cause separation. It can also be an effort to maintain closeness with other living loved ones about whom a client may feel inordinate fears and excessive worry.

DISCUSSING GRIEF ANXIETY

Regardless of their general behaviors or the specific types and manifestations of their grief anxiety, clients possess important insights into their experiences with both grief and anxiety. To best support clients as they begin to identify and understand grief anxiety, consider the questions that follow

Some clients may find it difficult to answer these questions or discuss their anxiety more generally. In fact, many people become more anxious when they talk about their anxiety, even if they aren't also grieving. For these clients (and for many others), it can be useful to slowly work through each question, pausing for regulating exercises, which will be covered in the next section. It may also be useful to show clients a list of common physical or behavioral symptoms of anxiety, or you can also provide education about the relationship between loss, fear, and anxiety so they feel equipped with the vocabulary to answer these questions.

 QUESTIONS FOR CLIENTS

Let's explore your anxiety:

- When did your anxiety start?
- Did this anxiety occur before the loss or only since the loss?
  - If since the loss, when did it first begin?
  - If before the loss, are there any notable differences in your anxiety since the loss?
- When do you feel anxious? All the time or intermittently?
- How does your anxiety manifest? (e.g., panic attacks, hypochondria, social isolation)
- What are some helpful strategies you've used to manage your anxiety thus far (e.g., journaling, deep breathing)?
- What are some unhelpful strategies you've used to manage your anxiety thus far (e.g., overeating, smoking, drinking)?
- What environments feel safe and soothing to you?
- What environments cause anxiety?
- In what ways does anxiety affect your life? (e.g., relationships, work, family)
- Are you taking medication for anxiety? If so what? For how long?

CHALLENGES TO NORMALIZING GRIEF ANXIETY

We all experience small amounts of anxiety all the time. In these moments, it serves as a reminder to adequately prepare ourselves or to stay alert. It is not until our anxiety begins to interfere in our day-to-day functioning—when, for example, we experience disruptive cognitive symptoms like a fear of being able to cope, or when we experience troubling behavioral symptoms like agitation we can't soothe or difficulty speaking—that we need to take measures to get our anxiety in check.

It can be a challenge to normalize an experience that feels so imminently dangerous. The physical and emotional symptoms of grief anxiety often manifest within the safe space of a session, causing extra panic. But you can provide relief to clients by helping them understand how common anxiety is, how anxiety works, how it manifests, and how it can be better managed and controlled.

ADDRESSING ANXIETY IN SESSION

Too many clients experiencing grief anxiety feel that there is something wrong with them or something wrong with the way they are grieving. These feelings can and do worsen symptoms associated with anxiety, including but not limited to anxiety about anxiety, isolation or detachment, and persistent helplessness or hopelessness.

After I conduct my observations at intake and ask my client questions, I usually draw on my own experiences to remind clients that anxiety can be a useful tool. Depending on what you described in your preparatory reflections, you may be able to use examples from your own life to describe anxiety's utility.

It is also important to help clients determine the difference between normal and abnormal anxiety.

Normal vs. Abnormal Anxiety

Normal Anxiety	Abnormal Anxiety
Can be attributed to a specific stressor	Source is unclear
Subsides when issue is resolved or slightly after	Intense feelings persist after issue is over
Does not interfere with daily functioning	Interferes with daily functioning
Limited physical symptoms	Multiple physical symptoms

The challenges associated with normalizing grief anxiety must be managed—not only to facilitate a client's ability to move through their grief process, but also to enable clients to function more comfortably in the here and now. I include a few quick tools here because it is important to offer support that clients can use *right away*, particularly if they recognize that their own anxiety is abnormal. You can find a more comprehensive list of anxiety exercises in chapter 9.

The following tools are accessible and easy to implement. They can be used when clients express anxiety at any point in their session:

- **Progressive muscle relaxation:** Progressive muscle relaxation helps to relax muscles through a two-step process. Instruct your clients to begin by tensing particular muscle groups in their body, such as their neck and shoulders. Next, have them release the tension and notice how their muscles feel when they relax them. This exercise helps to lower overall tension and stress levels and helps ease anxiety.

- **Diaphragmatic breathing:** Abdominal—or diaphragmatic—breathing can quickly reduce anxiety. Instruct your client to find a comfortable, quiet place to sit or lie down. Have them place one hand on their chest and the other hand on their belly, and allow their abdomen to relax without forcing it or clenching their muscles. Have the client breathe in slowly through their nose. The air should move into their nose and downward so that they feel their stomach rise with their other hand and fall inward (toward their back). Have them exhale slowly and take note of the hand on their chest, which should remain mostly still. Repeat this for five to ten minutes.

- **Compassionate self-talk:** When anxiety strikes, many clients tend to criticize themselves in the moment. This only makes them feel worse, upset, on edge, and more anxious. The key to using compassionate self-talk is for the client to pick specific phrases that feel meaningful and authentic to them. Try introducing phrases such as: *I am safe. I am healthy. I am calm. I am supported. It's okay that I'm having a hard time. I am doing the best I can.* It can also be effective to close your eyes and put your hands over your heart as you recite the phrases, as a small way to shut out the noise of the external world and reconnect with yourself.

MANAGING PANIC ATTACKS IN SESSION

Because talking about anxiety can sometimes provoke further anxiety, including panic attacks, it's important to be prepared to respond to symptoms of panic attacks that may arise during session.

For clients who appear to be experiencing symptoms of anxiety or panic during sessions, offer the following tips and guidance. Consider actuating the options that your clients identify as helpful. For instance, you might turn on a lavender oil diffuser, provide your client a glass of ice water, or accompany your client on a short walk during session. Some other options may include:

- Reminding clients that their symptoms will pass

- Guiding clients in taking slow, deep breaths

- Suggesting a change of environment

- Encouraging clients to tap into their senses, such as smelling lavender or holding an ice cube in their hand

- Identifying a helpful mantra that can be repeated

- Suggesting a short walk or light exercise, such as stretches

- Offering your clients an object, such as a snow globe, to focus on

REFLECTION

Grief anxiety can pose significant complications for grieving clients. But it is both common and manageable. As with the grieving process, helping clients to understand and normalize their experiences of grief anxiety enables them to accept, feel, and then process that grief anxiety. This is necessary to help clients move through their grief process, but it's also necessary to help clients function more comfortably in their day-to-day lives.

CHAPTER 6

APPROACHING FAMILY, WORK, AND LIFESTYLE DYNAMICS

Grief is a curious thing when it happens unexpectedly.
It's a band-aid being ripped away, taking the top layer off a family.
And the underbelly of a household is never pretty, ours is no exception.

—Jodi Picoult

Grief has universal traits, but it looks different for each person. Distinctions in each client's families, relationships, and professional and personal experiences, past and present, all inform their experience of loss. Consequently, getting to know the broader scope of your clients' lives, including their family dynamics and their work and lifestyle experiences, is vital to understanding how to best support them.

Sometimes it's easy to get a full picture of a client's present life circumstances and the past from which they've emerged from their story of loss. Other times, you can get this story from client questions and activities undertaken in the service of normalizing grief and grief anxiety. But in some circumstances, this information must be sought out in more targeted ways.

In these cases, I like to begin by first getting to know the full scope of a client's present life before digging into their past. The initial sessions are often consumed with listening to the client's story of loss, helping to stabilize them in their grief, and providing education to normalize their grief and grief anxiety. After this work has been established, it's time to begin to understand the bigger picture.

In this chapter, I describe the work of approaching family dynamics and family-of-origin issues through attachment styles. I then discuss how to approach work and lifestyle dynamics with grieving and anxiously grieving clients. A client's work and professional life poses a number of challenges to the grief process and is an important variable in their grieving process. I therefore discuss these challenges and offer a few tools that can be used to address difficulties related to personal and professional dynamics.

APPROACHING FAMILY DYNAMICS IN GRIEF

Family dynamics are a critical input to your clients' grieving process. Generally speaking, family dynamics investigates the patterns of interactions among relatives and at the varied factors that shape their interactions. Because family members rely on each other for emotional, physical, and economic support, they are one of the primary sources of relationship security or stress in your clients' experience of loss and grief.

Some clients have solid and supportive family dynamics. These clients can and should rely on family members to help them heal and process grief. Other clients may have fractured families or more challenging dynamics. This can result in family members who are unable to support one another in the grieving process. A lack of support can have deeper impacts as well. In extreme cases, a lack of support can delay or prevent a grieving individual from being able to heal in their grief, or it can block a person's progress in their grieving process. Family conflicts can even sometimes perpetuate grief, prolonging the grieving process or making it more complicated in other ways.

Whether their families are supportive and strong or fractured and dysfunctional, your clients will benefit from your assistance in navigating some of the family-based challenges that can arise during the grieving process.

To turn a client's attention to the impact of their family connections and personal support network on their grieving process, start a discussion with them using the following questions. The answers will provide you both with insight into their support system, including its strengths and weaknesses. As your client talks through their answers, you can help them consider who among their family members are most, and perhaps least, capable of offering support.

 QUESTIONS FOR CLIENTS

Let's consider your current support network:

- With whom are you the closest to?
- With whom do you feel the most supported?
- With whom do you have the most difficult or challenging relationships?
- With whom do you feel most comfortable grieving?
- With whom do you wish you could spend more time?
- With whom do you feel the most uncomfortable grieving around?
- Are any of these relationships a source of anxiety?
- How do the people in your life expect you to grieve?

UNDERSTANDING FAMILY-OF-ORIGIN DYNAMICS

A client's current relationships, both within their family and within their larger network of support, have been influenced (and likely continue to be influenced) by the dynamics that characterized their family of origin. In fact, a client's past experience with their family of origin can shed light on the person that seeks support in grief today.

To better understand a client's family-of-origin dynamics, ask them to describe their family of origin, and then use the prompts that follow to encourage further discussion or to facilitate your client's further reflection.

The client may find some of these questions easy to answer, and they may find others difficult to discuss. Some answers may point to relationship dynamics that are worthy of further investigation, particularly in the context of loss and grief. For example, clients who struggle to allow some of the more vulnerable emotions associated with grief, especially emotions that are unexpected or that don't seem to adhere to a recognized model, may describe families of origin in which emotions were not welcome. Exploring the possibility of a connection between their current grief and their family dynamics may provide a client insight into their grieving process.

Whether or not the connections between the client's current experiences of grief and family of origin are clear, their responses to these questions provide a context against which their experience of grief can be understood.

 QUESTIONS FOR CLIENTS

Let's consider your family-of-origin experiences:

- Who was your closest caregiver when you were young?
- What made you feel loved and cared for?
- Did you ever feel unsafe? When?
- What were you taught about emotions?
- Did you ever witness your parents experience grief?
- What are your parents' backgrounds?
- What is your relationship like with your siblings?
- What is something you wish you had when you were young?

INTERPRETING ATTACHMENT THEORY AND GRIEF

In my work with grieving clients, I use attachment theory as a tool for understanding their family dynamics and the impact of their families of origin on their current relationships. Your clients' attachment style informs the relationships in their lives, and when they grieve, their attachment systems can also inform the ways they are impacted by loss.

Attachment theory focuses on the relationships and emotional bonds between people, including those between a parent and child and between romantic partners. Psychologist John Bowlby, the first attachment theorist, determined that the earliest bonds that children form with their caregivers have a tremendous impact that continues throughout their lives. Essentially, the amount of protection and comfort a child receives or does not receive from their early caregivers affects their later participation in relationships.

A person's attachment system can indicate a lot about their grief. At the same time, experiencing loss can also disrupt a person's attachment system. It is therefore helpful to understand the basics of the four attachment styles and to consider how they relate to the grieving process.

Secure Attachment

People with secure attachment styles appreciate their own self-worth and are able to be in intimate relationships. They are comfortable expressing feelings, hopes, and needs. They find satisfaction in being with others but do not get overly anxious when they are apart from loved ones.

When an adult with a secure attachment experiences a significant loss, it is not likely to skew their preexisting attachment style, and a typical response to loss is to be expected. If the grieving person experiences anxiety following the loss, it is likely to be temporary. However, if a child or adolescent experiences the loss of a caregiver, their secure attachment system could be disrupted.

Adults with secure attachment systems can be supported through talk therapy that includes processing of anger and guilt, and pursuing the broader, deeper meanings of their experiences.

Anxious-Ambivalent Attachment

People with an anxious-ambivalent attachment system tend to be overly needy and anxious about separation. They crave intimate relationships but struggle to trust partners and friends. They can become overly fixated on other people, find it difficult to observe boundaries, and experience fear and paranoia of abandonment. They may also feel anxious and jealous when away from partners and may use manipulative tactics to keep them close. They often struggle to maintain close relationships.

When someone with an anxious-ambivalent attachment system experiences a loss, they are likely to experience an uptick in their anxiety levels. They may develop heightened fears around separation or worries about losing someone else. They may also become clingier and needier than usual with the people around them.

A person with anxious-ambivalent attachment styles who has experienced a loss can often be supported with strategies for self-soothing, such as psychoeducation around grief and attachment and anxiety management. This is particularly useful when anxiety flares. Additionally, in therapy, circling back to early experiences of separation can be helpful when anticipating potential sources of anxiety and upset, as well as identifying effective solutions.

Avoidant Attachment

People with avoidant attachment styles typically find it difficult to tolerate emotional intimacy. They value their independence and freedom to the point where they may feel uncomfortable and stifled by intimacy and closeness in relationships. The closer or needier another person becomes, the more a person with an avoidant attachment style tends to withdraw. In general, they are uncomfortable with their emotions. They may crave close, meaningful relationships but struggle to overcome their fears of intimacy.

When a person with an avoidant attachment experiences a loss, they may withdraw further from their close relationships and tend toward isolation in their grief. Their fears of abandonment are typically activated by their loss, which means their attachment system is often a factor in their grief. Working with grieving clients with an avoidant attachment system may require more time in order to build trust within the therapeutic dynamic, resiliency techniques for social support, and psychoeducation around attachment and grief.

Disorganized Attachment

People with disorganized attachment styles frequently feel they don't deserve love or closeness in a relationship. They likely never learned to self-soothe their emotions, so relationships can feel frightening and unsafe. If they experienced abuse as a child, they may try to replicate the same abusive patterns of behavior as an adult. They may find intimate relationships confusing and unsettling, and they often swing between emotional extremes of love and hate for their partner. They may be insensitive and controlling. While they crave the security and safety of a meaningful relationship, they may feel unworthy of love and are terrified of getting hurt again.

When a person with a disorganized attachment style experiences a loss, they may show a wide spectrum of reactions, including avoidance and anxiety. A grieving client with disorganized attachment, may also harbor anger toward the person who died because they feel abandoned. Finding ways to help these clients feel stable and secure in their lives will be a work in progress.

Your clients' relationships are important to their experiences, and their family dynamics, family-of-origin issues, and attachment styles fundamentally inform their relationships. When a client's loved one dies, some of their relationships must serve an actively stabilizing, supportive role. This is why it is so important to explore family issues and attachment styles with individuals who have experienced loss.

APPROACHING WORK AND LIFESTYLE DYNAMICS IN GRIEF

Grieving clients require different types of support from different relationships. While their needs can be understood against the background of their family and family of origin, their needs should also be understood against the background of their lifestyles, both professional and personal.

DISCUSSING GRIEF AND THE WORKPLACE

Over the course of your work with grieving clients, you will become familiar with the hardships imposed on grieving individuals by the American workplace. The truth is, bereavement leave in the United States is almost nonexistent. On average, jobs offer up to three days off for their clients to respond to the loss of a loved one, regardless of their readiness to return to work.

Grieving and anxiously grieving clients can experience all kinds of practical difficulties associated with an "authorized" bereavement period—or even the lack of workplace policies all together. Naturally, a client's experiences are determined by their work situation and their relationship to their work. Some clients may feel a great deal of pressure to return to work or to fulfill their professional obligations. Others may feel their jobs no longer matter, and they may avoid going back to work. Some may be facing new financial realities as a result of their loss and may need to quickly find new work, including entering the workplace after many years away from it.

Regardless of the specifics of their situation, clients can struggle to integrate their new identity as a grieving person into their established identity as a working person. The culture of the American workplace culture often reinforces this struggle by inadvertently—or advertently—discouraging displays of grief. Further, the general discomfort with death and loss in society can mean that some coworkers are unable or unwilling to act as supportive listeners to a grieving colleague.

Given these challenges, a grieving client may face a number of obstacles as they return to the workplace following their loved one's death. Sometimes, they may be completely unable to integrate their grieving and working identities. In these cases, clients can still learn skills for managing and coping with their grief. Therapists and mental health professionals play a key role in helping to support clients as they acquire these skills.

How your clients approach the relationship between their grief and their workplace is informed by a number of variables. For instance, a client might feel pressure to perform at work or to find a new job. They might feel a desire to completely immerse themselves in work or, alternatively, to avoid work completely. A client may also alternate between a willingness and an unwillingness to acknowledge their loss or their new identity as a grieving person in their workplace. They may feel unable or unwilling to experience grief on the job, or they may feel barred from doing so.

To begin to identify what specific variables impact a client's grieving process and inform their ability to manage and cope with their grief in their workplace, start a discussion with your client using the questions that follow.

 QUESTIONS FOR CLIENTS

Let's consider how your grief has affected your work:

- Are you working?
- How your work impacted by this loss?
- Do you feel supported in your grief by your superiors?
- Are you able to take time off?
- Does your work cause you anxiety?
- Are there changes to your career that you need/want to make?
- If you are not working, do you need to begin working?

As you and your clients discuss their answers, you can begin to identify the ways that their workplace is—and is not—able to meet their needs as they grieve. While identification is not mitigation, identification is the first step toward handing back to your clients a sense of control about their experience of loss as it manifests in their work environment.

Let's pause for a moment to spend a bit of time on this issue of control. As discussed in previous chapters, the death of a loved one results, for many clients, in a feeling of radical helplessness. The grieving process can extend or deepen this feeling by subjecting people to emotions, feelings, behaviors, and even physical symptoms that they may not expect and do not always feel they can command. On top of this, many workplaces can exacerbate these feelings of helplessness by closing off options for their inevitable expressions of grief.

When you help clients identify the needs posed by their grief and then consider their workplaces' readiness to meet those needs, you support them as they take a step toward regaining some of the control that death and grief wrested away from them. You can help guide your clients toward the next steps by helping them identify methods for proactively managing and coping with their grief at work.

MANAGING GRIEF IN THE WORKPLACE

It's important to work toward creating a plan that your clients can use to manage grief and cope with its inevitable irruption in the workplace. Encourage clients to examine their expectations around their workload, their coworkers, and potential grief triggers. Facilitate an in-session conversation about these expectations using the following questions. You can use their answers to inform a discussion about useful coping strategies.

 QUESTIONS FOR CLIENTS

Let's think about your current comfort level at your job:

- How much work do you think you can handle?
- How comfortable are you talking to your boss/supervisor about your grief?
- How comfortable are you asking for help?
- What are the grief triggers at your job?

Exploring potential answers to the preceding questions can help your clients to set expectations—both for themselves and for their workplace—before problems arise. Of course, setting expectations will not alleviate pain or discomfort. Regardless of expectations, it's very likely that grieving clients will, at some point, feel overwhelmed at work. It's also very likely that they will experience discomfort with asking for help at work. Preparing clients for these uncomfortable experiences can help them externalize workplace overwhelm and discomfort as part of the grieving process, rather viewing this distress as a personal failing.

COPING STRATEGIES FOR GRIEF IN THE WORKPLACE

The previous questions will help clients to identify and prepare for some of the challenges posed by the incongruence between their experience of grief and their experience as a working individual. However, taking steps toward managing their grief in the workplace requires clients to identify a handful of coping strategies they can use when in need of more support.

Introduce these accessible coping strategies to your clients as part of your broader conversation about grief in the workplace:

- **Ask for help and communicate with coworkers:** Requesting help is a valuable skill for all individuals, but it is necessary to the well-being of those who have experienced loss. Clients simply cannot absorb the impact of their loss on their own as it manifests through the grieving process. Asking for help when they need it is essential. Support your clients by practicing workplace scenarios in which they must ask others for help. This work can help expand their relative comfort in asking for help in other contexts.

- **Avoid overexertion and take frequent breaks:** In the context of work, clients may want to push through, or they may find that they can position work as an escape from other elements of grief. However, these habits can lead to overwhelm and burnout. There is no "other side" of the grieving process, nor can the grieving process be paused. There may be times when it appears dormant, but it affects clients whether they are aware of the effect or not. Explain to your clients that closure depends in part on their expression of grief. Taking frequent breaks at work is one way to cope with challenging feelings.

- **Use time off wisely:** For reasons I've described in previous chapters, is important for clients to identify the anniversaries and holidays that lie ahead. For instance, a loved one's birthday might be a particularly challenging day at work, so it might be a day that clients prefer to spend outside of work. Rather than divide their focus at work, potentially turning away from the inevitable feelings of grief that arise on difficult anniversaries and holidays, they can plan in advance how to acknowledge the day. To support clients, help them identify important anniversaries and holidays in the coming year. Consider working to create a plan for managing their work schedule on these days.

- **Create a back-up plan:** Despite your clients' best intentions and well-laid plans, grief will erupt when they are not prepared for it. Prepare clients for this reality by helping them to create a workplace-specific plan. It might mean establishing an agreement with a supervisor that allows clients to take a few minutes away from work duties when the need arises. During this time, clients may keep a short list of loved ones whom they can call at a moment's notice. They may also practice one or two regulating exercises, such as diaphragmatic breathing, to self-soothe.

While the preceding strategies cannot take away the grief clients will feel in the workplace, it can help them feel prepared for it, and therefore, feel a bit more in control.

Discussing Housing and Financial Stability

Family dynamics and workplace dynamics will have a big effect on your clients' grieving process. So too will their home life, their financial status, and their place in their larger community. The loss of a loved one will often change the way that a client relates to these areas of their life. The changes are not always anticipated, nor are they typically welcome, and they can complicate the grieving process and provoke a great deal of anxiety.

To uncover lifestyle issues impacting your client's experience of loss, consider using the following questions as the basis for a broad discussion.

 QUESTIONS FOR CLIENTS

Let's consider how your loss has affected your lifestyle:

- How has the loss impacted your home life and living situation?
- How has the loss impacted your financial status?
- How has the loss impacted the location of where you live?
- Are there changes to your home that you need or want to make?

It is not unusual for clients to experience a secondary loss, such as the loss of income or property security, subsequent to a loved one's death. In fact, some clients not only lose income but are saddled with medical bills or other costs associated with caretaking.

For some clients, however, their financial situation may have improved: They may be the recipient of an inheritance or a life insurance policy that increases their financial status. This may not feel like a windfall to most clients, however. While some may feel relief in new financial security, others feel pain or guilt about the change in their financial status and the loss that brought it about.

It is also common that clients a change in housing after the death of their loved one. Some are forced to downsize or to relocate due to changes in their financial situations. Others may have to move because they were living somewhere temporarily as a caregiver. On the other hand, some clients may choose to find a new home. For example, they may want to move closer to their support system, or perhaps it is too difficult to remain in the home they once shared with their loved one.

Although their individual circumstances may vary, clients require support when facing major changes to housing and financial stability. Some of this support is logistic: There are many different tasks that must be completed in order to find new housing and relocate. Some of this support is emotional: Moving after a loved one's death can be a painful secondary loss—and a highly symbolic one—for many clients.

To support clients as they navigate these changes, consider possible referrals to outside sources of support, like financial planners who can help with goal setting. You may also consider offering your clients the techniques of resiliency, which can be found in more detail in chapter 12.

UNDERSTANDING HEALTH, EXERCISE, AND SUBSTANCE USE

I always ask my grieving clients about their health and their relationships to exercise, medications, and substances. There are so many things that can impact a client's ability to process emotion, and their ability to grieve and handle anxiety can be predicated on some of these factors.

Accordingly, in the early sessions of our work together, when I am learning more about a client's family dynamics, workplace dynamics, and financial situation, I also ask about their physical health.

 QUESTIONS FOR CLIENTS

Let's focus on your physical health:

- How would you describe your health?
- When was your last checkup?
- How often do you exercise?
- Are you on any medications?
- What's your relationship with alcohol?
- Do you use drugs such as marijuana or other substances?
- What do you do to take care of yourself?
- Is there anything regarding your health you are worried about?
- How do you feel your grief and anxiety are impacted by your health, exercise, and substance use?
- Are there any changes you want to make to any of your previous answers?

SIMPLE WAYS TO TAKE CARE OF YOURSELF

For some clients, just taking a few steps to care for their physical well-being is enough. Others may need to consult a doctor or make more effort to increase their health. Regardless, for most clients, a simple cheat sheet like the one below can be an incredibly useful reminder of the more basic, easy-to-implement building blocks for better health and a stronger mind-body connection.

The following are simple self-care activities that almost any client can do to increase their well-being. Though it may seem tough during the grief process, grieving and anxiously grieving clients will especially benefit from incorporating the following into their routines:

- **Exercise:** Taking walks or doing some form of cardio can help calm your nervous system and induce helpful endorphins.

- **Do yoga:** Yoga offers a wonderful way to soothe your body and get centered when you are grieving.

- **Meditate:** Meditation is one of the best practices for calming your nervous system and escaping from anxious thoughts or rumination.

- **Get enough rest and sleep:** Getting a good night's sleep—and making time to rest separately from sleeping—is vital and will help you regulate your emotions.

- **Eat a nutritious diet:** Making sure your body is getting enough nutrients will also help ease feelings of irritability and exhaustion. Many people who are grieving experience a loss of appetite. If necessary, try drinking smoothies or protein shakes to fuel your body. Again, this will help you to withstand the intense emotions you are experiencing.

- **Take vitamins and supplements:** Bolstering your immune system during this time is important.

- **Stay hydrated:** Hydration is important to your bodily functions and can help you feel more balanced.

- **Journal:** Writing—especially noting your current feelings or capturing your current experiences—is a helpful practice for stress and anxiety.

- **Avoid alcohol and drugs:** These are easy coping mechanisms to turn to when you are grieving, but they can exacerbate anxiety, sadness, depression, and irritability.

REFLECTION

Family, work, finances, lifestyle: All of these inputs affect your clients' grieving journey. Understanding the stressors and supports that characterize each input will help to inform your course of care. When clients are able to identify these stressors and supports, they are able to avoid known stressors and rely on useful supports. This empowers clients and readies them to better cope with and manage the different aspects of the grieving process ahead.

CHAPTER 7

UTILIZING MINDFULNESS
AND MEDITATION

Meditation takes us just as we are, with our confusion and our sanity.
This complete acceptance of ourselves as we are is called maitri, or unconditional
friendliness, a simple, direct relationship with the way we are.

—Pema Chödrön

I once believed that mindfulness and meditation were inaccessible to someone like me. My thoughts were always racing through my mind, dominating my every waking moment. Surely, meditation practices were only available to those who had already achieved a certain level of *namaste*. They certainly didn't seem to be available to me.

I began to think differently in my late twenties, when, after a few years of intensely grieving the death of my parents, I was ready to lean into a different way of life. A friend recommended that I experiment with meditation. I knew that for her, establishing a meditation practice had been life-changing. Seeing its obvious impact on her, I knew I wanted to give it a try.

I found a teacher and began to work toward a practice. Yet, after several weeks of increasing frustration, I was about ready to give up. I found the process of meditation confounding. I had assumed that with a little effort, I'd be closer to the mystical yogi on the mountaintop, effortlessly contemplating life from a full-lotus position. But I was no contemplative yogi. The more I tried to turn off and turn away from my thoughts, the more they insisted on being noticed.

When I expressed my frustration to my teacher, she nodded knowingly. She encouraged me to view meditation not as a practice of exertion or achievement, nor as the peaceful contemplation of emptiness. Instead, she said, meditation is nothing less than the practice of observing our thoughts—*all* of our thoughts—with compassion.

When I realized that I didn't have to try quite so hard to stop thinking, that I could focus on noticing my thinking instead, I began to learn a few important and enduring truths. First, I learned that I am not my thoughts, and the thoughts I have are not me. This sounds so simple, but for me it was a radical truth: No matter how mundane or miserable my thoughts, they are separate from who I am.

Second, I learned that my thoughts triggered emotional and physical responses in my body. When I saw myself as an extension of my thoughts, my thoughts took on outsized power and importance. Wrapped up in their effects, I felt like I was on an emotional rollercoaster and couldn't get off the ride. However, when I began to separate myself from my thoughts, I was able to observe the effect my thoughts had on my emotional and physical responses from a more neutral distance.

Third, the more I practiced observing my thoughts and the more neutrally I was able to observe them, the more curious I became about them. The more curious I became, the more my thoughts, whatever they were, were able to simply come and go. Rather than feeling trapped by their power, I was able to allow my thoughts to rise and fall like my breath, feeling compassion for myself despite the emotional or physical response they triggered.

Over time and with practice, meditation became a profoundly freeing experience for me. My thoughts hadn't changed at all, but I had changed my relationship to them. The more I saw them as neutral, the more I let them flow through me, the less power they exerted over me, and the more space I gained simply to be myself.

Now, when I reflect on my journey through grief, I see mindfulness and meditation as a crucial part of my journey. They are not only much more accessible than the yogi's mountain, but they're also two of the most powerful tools you can give clients as they grieve.

In this chapter, I discuss how to introduce and implement mindfulness and meditation to grieving clients. First, I define mindfulness and meditation. Then, I describe how to introduce the concepts and begin to practice aspects of mindfulness and meditation with clients. Next, I introduce and describe activities and exercises that can be used to support clients as they begin to establish their own practices. My hope is to normalize mindfulness and meditation as a foundational component of grief and grief anxiety work, not only for clients but for therapists and mental health professionals too.

PREPARING FOR MINDFULNESS AND MEDITATION

Given my own experience and my experiences with clients, I consider practices in mindfulness and meditation the most useful tools for supporting clients as they learn to sit with some of the more difficult experiences of grief. This is particularly true for clients who are also dealing with grief anxiety.

Interestingly, I seldom have to persuade clients of this point: I've found that both grieving clients and anxiously grieving clients are typically very receptive to mindfulness and meditation. For some, they are willing to try anything that will give them even a little bit of space from their thoughts. For these clients, mindfulness and meditation practices often become instrumental to their healing journeys.

To encourage the exploration of the wide variety of mindfulness and meditation tools, it is useful to establish common definitions. This is especially the case with mindfulness. Whereas meditation is becoming a more mainstream practice in areas like sports and business, mindfulness depends on a broader concept and, for some, may feel more difficult to approach.

WHAT IS MINDFULNESS?

Mindfulness refers to a state of nonjudgmental awareness. We engage in mindfulness when we focus our attention on our perception in the present moment, using each of our senses to investigate and accept where we are in the here and now. Practicing mindfulness refers to the wide variety of techniques by which we foster this nonjudgmental awareness and train it on the present moment.

Typically, we practice mindfulness by focusing on the inputs of each of our senses. For instance, center yourself in this moment in part by asking yourself: What do you see? What do you hear? What do you smell? What can you touch? What do you taste?

WHY ARE MINDFULNESS AND MEDITATION USEFUL?

The thoughts that run ceaselessly through clients' minds can occupy so much of their attention that they constantly take them out of the present moment. These thoughts often feel incredibly powerful: With their associated emotional and physical triggers, they can even shape a client's sense of external reality. Yet, clients' thoughts are not always representative of external reality. In fact, their thoughts frequently keep them from experiencing the reality of the present moment as it is.

You can see an aberrant illustration of this in the client who struggles with paranoia or with more simple conspiratorial tendencies. When you talk with this client, you may observe that the thoughts they give expression to don't seem to correspond to your shared reality. Yet, you also see that their thoughts are so powerful that they have become, for the client, the only reality that matters.

Of course, it's not at all necessary to struggle with paranoia or conspiratorial tendencies to recognize the many ways your clients' thoughts contribute to, and even shape, their sense of reality. Many people find themselves beholden to an inner monologue that diverts their attention from present concerns. They may realize that they attend too closely to their internal thoughts and to the feelings and physical sensations they provoke. Clients may sense that they are missing many of the things that are happening outside their thoughts, even though these things are what make up their present life.

Mindfulness and meditation are not intended to stop a client's thoughts or to turn off their inner monologue. That is not possible. Instead, share with your clients that the practice of mindfulness and meditation is to refocus their attention toward their external experiences in the current moment. Often, activities that call attention to sense experiences help to practice mindfulness and meditation, and after some practice, these activities will enable clients to inhabit the current moment. By carefully focusing on their experiences of eating, breathing, and feeling the physicality of their bodies, clients can forge important connections to the here and now.

WHY SHOULD GRIEVING CLIENTS PRACTICE MINDFULNESS AND MEDITATION?

Like most practices in this book, mindfulness and meditation are useful for everyone, but they're especially beneficial for grieving clients. When they are grieving, they spend a lot of time thinking about the past. They think about how things used to be, about the times they spent with their loved one, and about the painful circumstances of their person's death. They also spend a lot of time thinking about the future. They will think about how they'll make ends meet, how they'll find the support they need, and about how they'll face anniversaries and other important dates.

Thoughts of the painful past and the unknown future trigger intense emotional and physical responses that can completely overwhelm clients, even powerfully shaping their experience of reality. For example, a grieving client who continually revisits the agonizing moment that they learned of their loved one's death continually renews their torment. It becomes a perpetually present pain. Mindfulness and meditation cannot take this pain away, but the practices can help them view their pain more neutrally, as one powerful experience among the many that shape their present reality.

For clients experiencing grief anxiety, mindfulness and meditation practices are even more critical. These clients also spend a great deal of time in the past and future, but their thoughts frequently trigger emotional and physical responses like anxiety and panic. When their thoughts result in the perception of a threat, their amygdala can become stimulated, which then readies the central nervous system for an attack.

Although the anxiety and panic felt by clients with grief anxiety results from the *feeling* that something is a threat, this threat is real from the client's perspective. In fact, clients with grief anxiety often cannot connect with themselves in the present because they are working so hard to defend themselves from the pain of the past and fear of the future.

Finding ways to focus your grieving clients' awareness on the present is important and can be incredibly helpful and calming. When grieving clients and clients with grief anxiety practice turning their attention toward their current experiences, tuning into their senses, and grounding in the here and now, they gain some distance from the past and future. When they get into the practice of observing their thoughts, they find that their thoughts do not require any reaction other than compassion. Rather than riding the rollercoaster of their feelings, these clients will begin to understand that they can *decide* to get off the ride.

ACTIVITIES TO HELP CLIENTS USE MINDFULNESS

The activities that follow encourage grieving clients to practice engaging mindfully with their present life. Although each activity may appear to be deceptively simply, many clients are not aware of the ways that their grief and grief anxiety dominate their thoughts and shape their experiences of the here and now. In practice, they may find some activities to be more difficult than anticipated. It's therefore useful to check in with clients about their experiences with these activities, perhaps even taking time in session to practice them, as necessary.

THE PRESENT MOMENT

The *Present Moment* activity is designed to support clients as they take the first step toward building their mindfulness and meditation practice. It is an activity in which clients are asked to sit still, observe their environment, and tune in to their thoughts.

As I mention above, it sounds simple, but many clients, especially those who experience grief anxiety, will struggle to focus their attention on the present moment. They may feel as though they can't engage with the activity until they can "turn off" their anxious feelings, or they may feel they cannot really engage with the present at all until they have their anxiety and panic under control. Luckily, this activity can be done with.

The *Present Moment* activity is not a one-time event. It's the beginning of a mindfulness practice that can help clients to break the cycle of anxiety-provoking thoughts. The practice will not stop their thoughts. In fact, it is important to communicate to clients that completing this activity and focusing on the present moment is not intended to stop their thoughts. It is designed instead to support them as they learn to observe and then interpret their thoughts in the safe context of the present.

To introduce this activity, guide clients through the exercise by first describing the purpose of mindfulness and meditation. Then, share a copy of the activity, and explain that it is designed to help bring clients into the present moment as fully as possible. Next, lead clients in the exercise by asking them to get comfortable and to bring themselves into the present by looking around the room and registering their feelings and sensations as you ask them a series of prompts.

IN-SESSION ACTIVITY

Read the following paragraph and answer the prompts to bring yourself into the here and now:

Look around the room in order to bring yourself fully into the present. Note the temperature and the way your body feels. Do you feel hungry? Thirsty? Hot? Cold? If your mind drifts to the past or to the future, that's okay. Just gently remind yourself that you are sitting in this room in the present, and this present is the only moment that exists. The past has already happened, and the future is not yet real.

- Right now, I see . . .
- Right now, I hear . . .
- Right now, I smell . . .
- Right now, I am touching . . .
- Right now, I feel . . .

MINDFUL EATING

The *Mindful Eating* activity is another useful method for introducing the concept of mindfulness to clients and encouraging its practice. In fact, integrating mindfulness into a daily activity like eating can be particularly helpful for clients because it can take out some of the guesswork around when, where, and exactly how to practice mindfulness. In fact, linking new habits to ingrained routines can make it easier to practice mindfulness regularly.

Additionally, the almost endless variety of tastes, textures, scents, and colors makes food an ideal object of sense-based exploration. Mindful eating is a novel practice for most people, but it is quite easy to begin and to repeat, and many people find it not only accessible but even enjoyable.

Introduce the *Mindful Eating* activity in session, preparing your clients for the activity by asking them to bring in a favorite food, such as an orange or a piece of chocolate. After guiding them through the activity, ask the client to experiment with this activity as they partake in meals over the course of your work together.

IN-SESSION ACTIVITY

Use the following steps as a guide to practice mindful eating:

1. Choose a small piece of food, such as an orange slice or a cookie.
2. Begin by examining the piece of food, using as many of your senses as possible. Look at the food, noticing its texture and color.
3. Next, close your eyes, and examine the food with your sense of touch. What does it feel like? Is it hard or soft? Rough or smooth? Wet or dry?
4. Before you put the food in your mouth, use your sense of smell to explore the food. What do you notice?
5. Now, start to eat. No matter how small the piece of food is, take at least two bites to consume it.
6. Chew your first bite very slowly, noticing the sensory experience of chewing and tasting. You might want to close your eyes for a moment to focus on the sensations before continuing.
7. Notice the way the food feels in your mouth.
8. Notice if the flavor changes, moment to moment.
9. Take about 20 more seconds to very slowly finish this first bite of food, being aware of all the sensations of chewing and tasting. You don't always have to eat slowly in order to eat with mindfulness. But it's helpful at first to slow down, so you can be as mindful as possible.
10. Next, continue eating and taking more bites. Continue to chew very slowly, while paying attention to the sensations and movements of chewing, the flavor of the food as it changes, and the sensations of swallowing. Just pay attention, moment by moment.

MINDFUL BODY SCAN

The *Mindful Body Scan* is a progression in mindfulness practice. Generally, this activity requires a bigger time commitment than the *Present Moment* activity, and it may not be as easy for clients to integrate it into their daily routines as *Mindful Eating*. However, body scans can help focus clients' awareness onto their bodies, especially its aches, pains, and acute or general discomforts.

Everyone stores anxieties and tensions in our bodies, but we may not realize this until we focus our attention on our different body parts. When, for instance, a client focuses their attention on their shoulders, they may become aware of a tightness in their shoulders, or they may realize that they're holding their shoulders near their ears. When they shift their attention to their jaw, they may become aware that they're clenching their teeth. The *Mindful Body Scan* directs your clients' awareness and breath to the different sensations in their bodies, teaching them to notice their discomfort while directing their breath to it.

It can be useful to introduce clients to the body scan in session, especially when they feel stressed or overwhelmed. Completing the activity during the session can help to calm clients and to show them the cadence and ideal pace of the activity. Once you have completed the activity during a session, send your clients home with the following handout and instructions to perform a body scan once a week.

MINDFUL BODY SCAN

This activity will help you turn your attention to various parts of your body in order to cultivate an awareness of the present moment and to create relaxation. Most people prefer to lie down or sit in a chair during a body scan, but feel free to experiment with what works best for you.

1. To start, find a comfortable position, either sitting or lying down. Close your eyes and uncross your arms and legs, feeling the support from the ground or the chair.

2. Notice your breath coming in and out of your body. Feel it enter through your nose or mouth, move through your chest, and fill your lungs. Then feel your breath moving out of your body. Continue to take a few moments to focus on your breath flowing in and out.

3. Next, bring your attention to your toes. Continue taking deep, slow breaths. Wiggle your toes slightly and focus your attention there.

4. Bring your attention to your feet. Continue to breathe deeply.

5. Bring your attention to your calves. How do they feel?

6. Bring your attention to your knees and move them gently.

7. Bring your attention to your thighs. Tense your thigh muscles, and then relax them as you continue to breathe deeply.

8. Bring your attention to your buttocks, squeezing them together and relaxing.

9. Bring your attention to your lower back. Notice any pain or tension there. Breathe deeply and let the muscles relax.

10. Bring your attention to your abdomen. Pay attention to its movement as you breathe in and out.

11. Bring your attention to your chest. Pay attention to its movement as you breathe in and out.

12. Bring your attention to your shoulders. Feel for any tension there and release it with your breath.

13. Bring your attention to your neck. Roll your head gently from side to side and relax the muscles.

14. Bring your attention to your face. Feel for any tension in your facial muscles and let it go as you continue to breathe.

15. Finally, bring your attention to your head and hair. Feel the weight of it and the air moving around it.

16. Continue breathing and release all of your body's tension. Enjoy the sensation of full body relaxation!

SQUARE BREATHING

No guide for mindfulness would be complete without instructions for deep, diaphragmatic breathing. *Square Breathing*, also known as box breathing, is a simple technique designed to help clients slow down their breath by breathing mindfully to the count of four. A diagram of a square often serves as a mnemonic, reminding clients to inhale for four counts, exhale for four counts, inhale for four counts, and finally, exhale for four counts. Square breathing is especially useful for clients who are struggling with grief anxiety. It can help to manage their anxiety symptoms by increasing their oxygen intake, lowering their heart rate, and calming their nervous system.

IN-SESSION ACTIVITY

Focusing on your breath helps you stay in the present moment. Use this breathing technique any time you become anxious or focused on a worrisome thought:

1. Inhale slowly through the nose for 4 counts.
2. Hold for 4 counts.
3. Exhale slowly through the mouth for 4 counts.
4. Hold for 4 counts.
5. Repeat for 5–10 minutes.

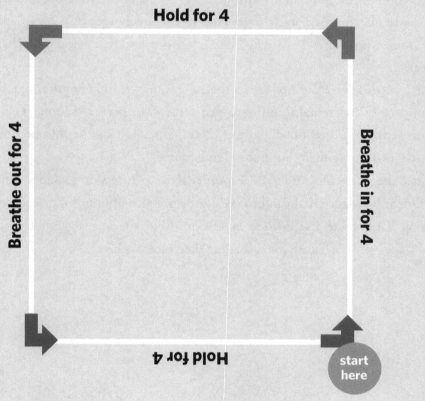

ACTIVITIES TO HELP CLIENTS USE MEDITATION

Whereas mindfulness helps foster the neutral awareness of all of our thoughts and feelings, meditation helps us to relax while also helping us become aware of our thought patterns, including intrusive thoughts and repetitive thinking. With meditation, clients can learn to shift their attention from thought patterns that do not serve them and stop further anxiety.

Meditation asks us to focus our attention on a specific thing, but many people assume that they can only do this if they also tune out everything else around them. People who bear the heavy load of grief often feel that their thoughts are disorganized, hard to control, or stuck in the past or future, especially their regrets, memories, and fears associated with life without their loved one. This can make meditation feel like a major challenge for grieving and anxiously grieving clients.

Just like in the context of mindfulness, it's important for therapists and mental health professionals to explain to clients that the goal of meditation is not to wholly tune out. The goal is instead for them to completely tune *in* to their point of focus—whether this is their breath, a specific word, or a mantra—in order to reach a calmer and more relaxed state.

MINDFUL MEDITATION

Clients may find meditation more intimidating than mindfulness because they think meditation requires a particular disposition, a particular type of technique, or a particular skillset. However, they must understand that they will benefit most from practicing mindfulness and meditation simultaneously.

In reality, meditation does not take a special person—it only requires a quiet place where clients can sit comfortably and remain uninterrupted for a short period of time. The goal of meditation is for clients to gently but intentionally direct their focus, allowing them to become aware of all of their thoughts, acknowledging them but not judging them.

Introduce the following *Mindful Meditation* activity in session to supply clients with an example of the rhythm and cadence that can be used in the practice of mindful meditation. Then, offer clients the following handout to use outside of session. Give them a suggested goal to practice mindful meditation once or twice before the next time they meet with you.

MINDFUL MEDITATION

Find a private, comfortable place where you can remain uninterrupted for a short period of time. Then, use these instructions to support your meditation practice. Do not worry too much about how much time to give yourself to meditate.

1. Set your timer for 5 minutes. If you are willing and feel comfortable, set your timer for 10 minutes.

2. Find a comfortable position, ideally one in which you won't feel the need to continually change positions.

3. Close your eyes.

4. Begin your meditation by bringing your awareness to the present moment.

5. Focus on the feeling of breath moving through your body.

6. Notice the way the air feels entering your nostrils and the way it feels exiting.

7. Your mind will wander and that is ok. You may grow bored or uncomfortable, and that's okay too.

8. Simply try to notice these sensations and any thoughts you might have as though you are an outside observer.

9. Accept your sensations and thoughts as part of your experience and return your attention to the present moment and the feeling of breath flowing in and out of your body.

10. Continue this process until your timer rings or until you feel ready to be finished.

EXPLORING MEDITATION

Although meditation doesn't require a special skillset, clients will need to practice in order to get the best results. Establishing a meditation practice can be challenging for a variety of reasons—just like the initiation of all new habits—but most reasons will be unique to each individual client. However, you know that as with any new behaviors, persistence matters: The more you practice it, the easier it becomes.

My experience with grieving clients and clients with grief anxiety has taught me that meditation is an invaluable tool. Depending on a client's needs and their experiences in adopting the mindful meditation practice, you may want to offer them further resources. There are many ways to deepen and to extend the practice of meditation. To support a client in starting their practice or in deepening it, you and the client may want to consult with a few knowledgeable resources. For example, the client may:

- Find a local meditation center or class.
- Join an online meditation program.
- Read books about meditation.
- Download a meditation app.
- Listen to podcasts about meditation.
- Attend a meditation retreat.

MEDITATION SCRIPT FOR ANXIETY

Although I discuss strategies for anxiety in chapter 9, anxious grieving is such a common challenge for clients coping with loss that I like to introduce meditation scripts to clients through this lens.

My choice is informed by the particular difficulties that anxiety poses for clients at the start of their meditation practice. In some ways, these difficulties are in an intensification of other grief expressions. For instance, the irregular irruption of anxiety symptoms can be unpredictable and all-consuming. Clients experiencing grief anxiety often feel helpless and out of control. Frequently, these clients may try to manage their feelings with hypervigilance, always on the lookout for signs of future anxiety or panic.

While this can feel like a major block to meditating, and especially to beginning a meditation practice, meditation is a particularly useful tool for addressing these symptoms. Meditation can help support all clients by showing them that they are not helpless and that they can gain control over their symptoms in a lasting way.

The following script teaches clients to slow down and focus on the feelings they're experiencing, as well as the feelings they're repressing. In particular, the script gently directs clients to focus in on their anxiety and fear. By guiding clients through this script during session, in a safe and therapeutic space, you introduce them to some of the healing benefits of meditation while helping them to take the first step toward a meditation practice. Consider recording the session and offering clients the recording for their use at home or whenever they want to benefit from focusing in on their anxiety and allowing its expressions to move through them.

 ## MEDITATION SCRIPT FOR ANXIETY

Close your eyes and begin to take slow, even breaths. Let any sounds fall away. Let any random thoughts just drift off. Simply focus on your breath and the sound of my voice.

[Pause]

To practice this meditation, I want you to acknowledge the anxiety and fear you are feeling. Notice where you feel it in your body. Notice the thoughts that arise. Let your thoughts drift away and continue to focus on your breath.

[Pause]

Allow yourself to feel that you are safe and protected. Allow your breathing to deepen and your body to feel supported. Imagine the feeling of being hugged or held and focus on that feeling as you continue to breathe.

[Pause]

Allow all fear and negative thoughts to dissipate with each breath you release. Each time you breathe in, imagine that you are breathing in love and support.

[Pause]

Now try to view yourself with compassion and kindness. View yourself as you would a friend or even a child. Feel love, compassion, and forgiveness for yourself. Continue breathing.

[Pause]

Continue to release any anxious or fearful thoughts and let yourself enjoy the feeling of relaxation and comfort. Breathe out anxiety and breathe in support. Recognize the safety and stillness of this moment and let it be one that will guide you through the rest of your day.

[Pause]

Slowly begin to deepen your breath and come back into your body. Take your time opening your eyes and returning to the room.

REFLECTION

If your clients gain just one tool from this book, let it be the practice of mindfulness and meditation. While every tool is useful and has its place in the grieving process, establishing a practice of mindfulness and meditation can help clients to neutrally view their emotions and feelings, to acknowledge the impact of those emotions and feelings on their bodies, and to extend to themselves compassion and support. Furthermore, mindfulness and meditation practices can be deepened and extended in innumerable ways to support *every* client that walks through your door as they navigate the ups and downs of life.

CHAPTER 8

STRATEGIES FOR GRIEF

Grief is like the ocean; it comes on waves ebbing and flowing. Sometimes the water is calm and sometimes it is overwhelming. All we can do is learn to swim.

—Vicki Harrison

Although grief and the grieving process are typically considered to be one and the same, I often find it useful to approach grief as a single part of the grieving process, not as the grieving process itself. In some ways, grief can be considered a container that holds the varied emotions, feelings, behaviors, and physiological symptoms that arise as your clients process loss. They will carry their grief throughout their lives, but what it holds will differ depending on their changing relationship to the loss.

The utility of separating grief from the grieving process depends, in part, on the power of externalization. Grief can be so large and capacious for some clients that it can be hard for them to recognize that they are separate from their emotions, feelings, behaviors, and symptoms. Sometimes, when a client's experience is upsetting, uncontrolled, or seemingly uncontrollable, they may even feel that there is something wrong with them. Mindfulness and meditation practices can certainly help, but clients must do more in order to process their grief. Educate your clients that they must not see grief as an internal darkness that divides them from themselves and others but as an external container that they must carry. In changing this view, they can gain the space they need to process their loss more fluidly.

In this chapter, I introduce a variety of activities for broadly supporting clients as they hold their grief. The activities can be used in session to support clients as they learn to handle their grief in different ways, or they can be helpful outside of session as formal exercises or informal prompts and invitations for guided exploration. Because you will explore your clients' grief in different ways in every session, the activities in this chapter help to set a strong foundation for targeted work on the specific challenges associated with their grief, many of which I will discuss in the chapters that follow.

ACTIVITIES TO HELP CLIENTS IDENTIFY AND UNDERSTAND THEIR GRIEF

The ability to externalize grief takes a client's internal, personal source of anguish and adds to it an *outer* experience that they can investigate and explore. In this way, the aim of externalization echoes the objective of mindfulness and meditation practices. Externalization offers a means to establish the distance required for introspection and reflection. It allows clients to gain the clarity necessary to see that they are not coterminous with the pain of their loss—nor are they an extension of that pain.

This is not to say that externalization decreases the suffering brought on by grief. As with mindfulness and meditation, it doesn't, at least not immediately. However, as clients learn to view grief as something separate and therefore different from them, it becomes something that they can view more neutrally. Clients can learn to approach it with curiosity and openness so as to understand and accommodate it.

The following activities encourage clients to view grief as a natural consequence of experiencing—and then processing—a loss. The activities prioritize identifying, describing, and naming grief's different manifestations, including grief anxiety. Such activities help position grief as an experience with its own character and expressions, and they also prompt clients' investigation and exploration of their grief, which helps to model the curiosity that's so useful to approaching grief more neutrally.

GRIEF INVENTORY

The *Grief Inventory* gives you and your clients broad insight into their experience of grief. It is a useful addition to early sessions, potentially after listening to a client's story of loss.

Completing and discussing the *Grief Inventory* together may also help you and your clients identify a model of grief that feels like a useful lens for approaching and making sense of the client's experiences. In fact, you may want to discuss a few of the models described in chapter 3 in tandem with the *Grief Inventory*.

Although completing the inventory early in the course of care establishes a strong foundation for work, repeating it in later sessions is enormously useful too. Repetition helps clients continue expressing curiosity about their grief. It also encourages them to identify patterns, potential triggers, and effective coping mechanisms. Repetition can help clients observe and name the ways they learn to accommodate their grief, to make space for it, and to seek support as they continue to process their loss. Consequently, after taking inventory of clients' grief in initial sessions, offer them the accompanying *Grief Inventory* worksheet to complete periodically over the course of care.

GRIEF INVENTORY

Answer the following questions, providing as much detail as possible, to gain a broad picture of your grief.

How long have you been grieving?

_____

_____

_____

How does your grief display?

_____

_____

_____

What are your predominant emotions?

_____

_____

_____

How has your grief evolved since the loss?

_____

_____

_____

Is there anything that makes you feel blocked?

_____

_____

_____

What parts of your grief are you most comfortable with?

_____

_____

_____

What parts of your grief are the hardest or scariest?

_____

_____

_____

What are you currently doing to let others know your feelings about your loss?

_____

_____

_____

What part did you have in the funeral or memorial of the person who died?

_____

_____

_____

Are there any things you wish you had done at the funeral that you were not able to do?

_____

_____

_____

What are you trying to do for yourself to assist with mourning the person who died?

_____

_____

_____

What is the difference between mourning and grieving? Why is it important for you to confront your grief and not bury it?

_____

_____

_____

What is one thing you are doing to distract yourself a in healthy way?

_____

_____

_____

What does it mean to have a continued relationship with the person who died?

_____

_____

_____

How has this death affected your identity? What changes have occurred since the death?

_____

_____

_____

How has the death impacted your anxiety level?

_____

_____

_____

How has this death affected you spiritually or religiously?

_____

_____

_____

How are your family members and friends supporting you through this grief journey?

_____

_____

_____

How are your family members and friends holding you back?

_____

_____

_____

What are some things you stopped doing after the death that you would now or someday like to continue?

_____

_____

_____

What are some things you are hopeful for in the future?

_____

_____

_____

GRIEF SENTENCES

The *Grief Inventory* casts a wide net, asking clients to reflect on the many different ways their grief is impacting their lives. To augment the inventory, it's often useful to capture a snapshot of a client's current experiences of grief.

The *Grief Sentences* activity not only enables clients to express their current experience of grief, but it also encourages them to focus on their current relationship to their loved one who has died. This relationship is an important part of a client's life, and it will continue to be important throughout their grieving process.

When clients lose someone they love, they don't always know how to relate to them after death. Though this is partly due to the suppression of grief in American culture, it's also due to the pain, confusion, and difficulty clients feel when they think about the radical and typically unwelcome change that death has forced upon the relationship they have with their loved one. For some clients, the changed nature of this relationship is too painful or too personal to discuss with family and friends. Further, this pain can be bidirectional, and others don't always know how to offer their support.

The *Grief Sentences* activity gives clients a structured opportunity to benefit from therapeutic support as they capture and reflect on the changing nature of their relationship to their loved one now that they have died. I will return to the topic of maintaining a connection to a loved one who has died in chapters 13 and 14, but completing and repeating this activity early and often supports this ongoing work.

As with the *Grief Inventory*, this activity can be repeated over multiple sessions. It's especially useful as a prompt to help direct therapeutic support. If your clients find the activity comforting, it can be used instead as a prompt for reflection and closure at the end of sessions.

IN-SESSION ACTIVITY

Let's reflect on your current experience of grief:

- Right now I feel . . .
- I feel the saddest when . . .
- The thing I miss most about the person who has died is . . .
- Since the loss, things have been different because . . .
- If I could say one thing to the person who has died . . .
- Something I learned from the person who has did is . . .
- Something I loved about the person who has died is . . .

EXPECTATIONS AND ASSOCIATIONS FOR GRIEF

As I've discussed in previous chapters, many clients seek support after a loss because they fear they're not grieving in the so-called right way—otherwise known as the way that is dictated by popular models. Although it's only natural that people overwhelmed by grief and grief anxiety would assume that they'll feel better or more at ease if they could only grieve in the "right" way, it's important for clients to realize that their grief will manifest in its own ways.

To help draw clients' attention to the difference (and the distance) between their expectations of grief and their actual experiences of grief, ask them to answer the questions below. Supporting clients as they reveal their expectations, and perhaps judiciously sharing information about the range of experiences you have seen as a clinician—and perhaps even felt as a grieving person—can help clients understand and accommodate the different ways that grief manifests.

The answers to the following questions should be solicited in early sessions to gain insight into a client's relationship to their grief. However, you should continue to periodically pose the questions throughout the course of care to gain a sense of the client's developing relationship to their grief.

 QUESTIONS FOR CLIENTS

Let's compare your expectations of grief to your actual experiences:

- What are your expectations for grief?
- Who are your role models for grief?
- What does grief look like?
- What is positive about grief?
- What is negative about grief?
- When is grief okay?
- Where is grief okay?
- How long are you allowed to grieve?
- How long would you like to grieve?

Once you have worked through some of the exercises in this section and gained a comprehensive overview of your clients' grief, you can move to more hands-on activities, such as the *Grieving Figures* and *Personification* activities. These activities ask clients to enter into a different kind of relationship with their grief, envisioning it as something outside of themselves or something with particular features and characteristics.

The following activities also ask clients to consolidate and draw connections between their internal and external experiences of grief. Such work can help them visualize the different forms of their grief and, in so doing, can help determine the kinds of care and attention each form requires.

GRIEVING FIGURES

The *Grieving Figures* worksheet offers a therapeutic tool that makes use of metaphor to encourage clients to view their grief as a multidimensional experience that looks different on the inside than the it does on the outside.

While in session together, offer clients the following worksheet and a variety of writing, drawing, and perhaps painting materials. Ask them to represent what their grief looks like on the inside *and* the outside by drawing expressions, using colors, and creating images. When they feel their grieving figures are complete, ask them to narrate their choices, reflecting in particular on the differences between their feelings of grief. Then, ask them what kinds of attention or measures of comfort these different expressions of grief might benefit from.

GRIEVING FIGURES

Use the figures below to illustrate how your grief looks like on the inside and on the outside.

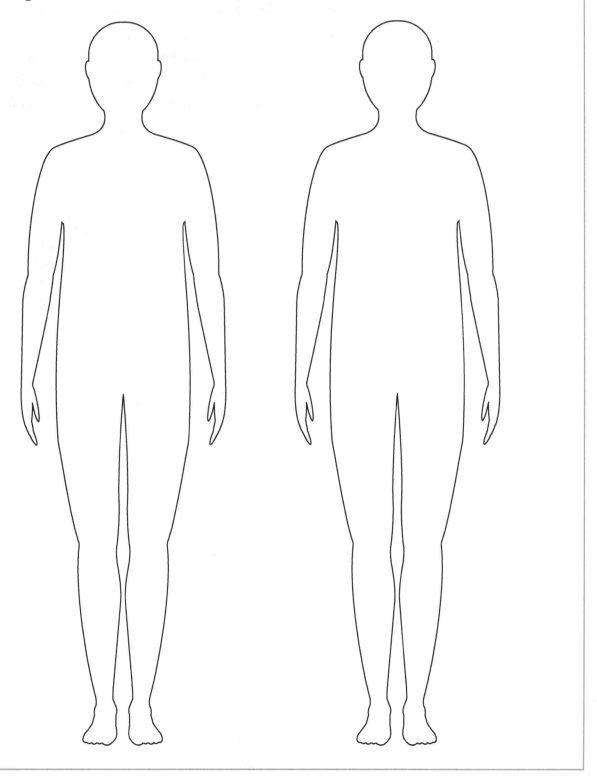

PERSONIFICATION

Much like the *Grieving Figures* worksheet, the *Personification* worksheet can help clients consolidate and externalize the different experiences of grief and make sense of death. In fact, consolidation aids externalization. When a client imagines their grief as a dynamic character, they may be more capable of approaching their grief as a partner with whom they must work—not as a parasite that threatens to subsume them.

Lead clients in this worksheet by asking them to imagine their grief as a character. Ask them to first describe this character. Is it an angry character, a sad character, a character that seeks to hide or run away, or a character who prefers to remain invisible? Is it a character who wants attention and affection, or who wants to yell and hit? Then, depending on this description, ask clients to give the character personality traits, hobbies and interests, strengths and weaknesses, and any other characteristics they feel help to explain their sense of their own grief.

Once they have described the personification of their grief, spend some time reflecting on what this personified grief may need or want and how your clients might want to respond.

GRIEF PERSONIFIED

Use the space below to draw your grief as a character with specific personality traits, hobbies and interests, strengths and weaknesses, and anything else you want to add.

MY GRIEF, MY WAY

Although the activities in this chapter do not need to be completed sequentially, *My Grief, My Way* is a culminating discussion and helps to direct some of the cumulative results from the previous activities. Consequently, before engaging with the questions below, clients should be able speak about the characteristics of their own grief, identify their own particular ways of grieving, and hold a fairly strong understanding that their grief is an experience that is unique to them and that will change over time.

As clients gain familiarity with their different expressions of grief, they also become more capable of thinking about the kinds of comfort and support that might be able to soothe these expressions. Then, as they gain confidence in their ability to identify potential means of comfort and support, they become more capable of feeling all of their different expressions of grief. This can be a virtuous circle. It's therefore important for clients to understand that their ability to identify and understand their different expressions of grief is just the beginning of moving more fluidly through their grieving process.

These questions can be approached as an in-session discussion, as a culmination of the preceding activities. You can also have clients fill out this information outside of session, which allots them more time for reflection. Consider introducing the questions in session and asking clients to revisit them in preparation for a later session.

 QUESTIONS FOR CLIENTS

To process loss, it is important to allow all of your expressions of grief to be expressed. To work toward this expression, answer the following questions with as much detail as possible:

- What are your ways of grieving?

    ◦ Emotionally . . .

    ◦ Physically . . .

    ◦ Practically . . .

    ◦ Socially . . .

- What rituals are important to you?
- What activities feel helpful to your grief?
- What routines are important to your grief process?
- What emotions are you comfortable displaying around others?
- What changes do you need to make to accommodate your grief?

ACTIVITIES TO HELP CLIENTS IDENTIFY THEIR GRIEF NEEDS

Once clients have experience in identifying their grief, you can begin to work with them to proactively identify and communicate their needs to others. It will come as no surprise to hear that communicating needs often poses a major challenge to clients. Identifying and communicating needs is a common challenge for grieving people and non-grieving people alike. However, for grieving and anxiously grieving clients, the challenge is exacerbated by the all-encompassing, intense nature of grief. These characteristics can make it hard to think of—and ask for—any one thing that could make grief better.

Some clients may be well aware of what they need after the loss of their loved one. They may have completed the preceding activities with ease. However, not all clients are able to state their needs or feel comfortable explaining those needs to others. At the same time, even when grieving people are able to articulate their needs, not all people are capable of meeting the needs of their grieving loved ones. For these reasons, clients may benefit from repeated practice in expressing their needs so that suitable members of their support network can meet them.

HOW OTHERS SPEAK TO US AFTER A LOSS

Many grieving people fear, or feel, that their support network is not up to the task of providing sustained help over the long grieving process. Sometimes, these fears are founded: As I discussed in chapter 1, it is the rare individual who is able to be a companion to grief. However, people who are grieving can and should still learn to ask for what they need. Although members of their support network may not know how to act as a companion to grief, they are frequently able to respond to needs that have been articulated. The more direct clients can be, the more likely their friends and their family will be able to respond.

For clients experiencing grief, understanding, identifying, and articulating their needs requires sophisticated communication skills. Some may take a long time to learn these skills. And after the death of a loved one, most people must relearn these skills in a new light. As a therapist or a mental health professional, you can prepare clients for the ways in which others, including family members and close friends, may interact with them. While the education imparts useful information, it also helps to keep clients from internalizing the less sensitive responses they may receive in response to their grief.

The following prompts open the door to further discussion, preparing clients for the activities in this chapter that will help them approach the subject of their loss and their needs around grief on their own terms. Introduce this as an in-session activity to collaborate with a client in generating a variety of different ideas and responses. You may also allow the client to reflect on their potential responses outside of session.

IN-SESSION ACTIVITY

Family members, friends, acquaintances, and strangers will likely all have different responses to your loss. Let's consider how the following hypothetical responses might affect you:

- Someone finds it difficult to talk to you about your loss and changes the subject.
- Someone avoids talking to you after your loss.
- Someone expects you to feel better and move on before you are ready.
- Someone does not know how to respond in the way you need.
- Someone says, "Aren't you over it yet?"
- Someone wants to talk about your loss past the point you are comfortable.
- Someone shuts you down or tries to cheer you up when actually, you still want to talk about it.

HOW TO TALK ABOUT YOUR LOSS

Clients often express the difficulties they feel in talking about their loss to others. Their grief may feel too big and life-altering for words. It may be that it feels too private to share with other people. In addition, their grief is always changing, so clients may feel that it is futile to express their experiences of grief in language. Despite these difficulties, a critical component of fully processing grief requires putting the experience of grief into words within the bounds of safe and comfortable relationships.

The *How to Talk About Your Loss* worksheet can help grieving clients work toward safe expression of their loss. It will help them to first identify if they *want* to share information about their loss and then to figure out what information they do and do not want to share.

The worksheet is divided into four sections:

1. Do I Want to Share?

2. How Can I Begin to Share?

3. What Are My Boundaries?

4. What About When I Don't Want to Talk about My Grief?

The first section is designed to help clients assess their comfort in talking about their loss with family members and close friends. Some of these prompts in this section may be difficult for clients to respond to, especially those concerning their boundaries. In this case, you may want to discuss the prompts and brainstorm potential responses in session, talking through clients' fears or anxieties around communicating about their loss and grief. It's important for them to understand that it's always their choice how, when, and with whom they want to talk about their loss—and that these decisions can change at any time. They need not justify their choice nor apologize for it.

The second section offers clients examples of conversation-openers to begin a discussion about their loss. Sometimes feelings and emotions can overtake a conversation, making it difficult to even begin talking about grief and loss. But remember that like most things, preparation and practice is key.

The third section helps clients identify their boundaries. Boundary work can be challenging for everyone, but it's especially difficult for grieving and anxiously grieving clients. In the discussion of boundaries with your clients, it is also important to mention the reality that boundaries can shift and change.

The fourth section gives clients an opportunity to practice communicating their boundaries. This preparation helps to communicate to clients that there will be times when they do not want to discuss their loss or their grief, and this is perfectly acceptable.

HOW TO TALK ABOUT YOUR LOSS

As your grief unfolds, your emotional landscape will fluctuate, as will your desire to talk about your loss. It's always helpful to check in with yourself before deciding to share your grief with others. Use this worksheet to talk about your grief with the people in your orbit.

1. **Do I Want to Share?**

    Remember that you are in control of the story of your loss. It is always up to you on how, when, where, and to whom you tell your story. To help you reflect on your decision to share, consider the following prompts:

    ○ Do I feel comfortable being vulnerable with this person?

    ○ Do I want to talk about my loss?

    ○ Do I feel this is the right moment and place for me to have this discussion?

2. **How Can I Begin to Share?**

    It can be hard to know how to begin discussing loss and grief because the feelings around them are often big, and they may feel unknown and uncontrollable. If this is the case for you, use the following prompts to help you get started. Once you've familiarized yourself with the preceding prompts and practiced them, write a prompt or two that you could use to talk about your grief with a friend or family member.

    ○ I've been having a hard time since my loss, and I'd like to talk about it.

    ○ It's hard for me to talk about surface things when I'm grieving. What I'd really like to share is . . .

    ○ My grief feels like . . .

    ○ It feels important for me to share a bit about my loss with you . . .

    ○ Talking about my loss is helpful, so I'd like to share it with you . . .

    ○ Ever since my person died my world has felt like . . .

    ○ _____

3. **What Are My Boundaries?**

   It's important to know that you can also choose to opt out of any conversation that feels overwhelming or disrespectful. This is not always easy, but you can make it easier by identifying your boundaries before the conversation arrives. To pinpoint the boundaries you have around your grief, consider the following prompts:

   What won't I tolerate?

   _____

   _____

   _____

   What triggers am I willing to address in the moment?

   _____

   _____

   _____

   What triggers are too charged to engage with?

   _____

   _____

   _____

4. **What About When I Don't Want to Talk About My Grief?**

   Boundary work is difficult work, and it is useful to have a few handy phrases to rely on, especially when conversations come up quickly or unexpectedly. Once you've gotten comfortable practicing the responses that follow, create one or two of your own responses that you can use when you are not ready to discuss your loss and grief. It's a good idea to practice these responses, either with family members or friends with whom you feel comfortable, or in a therapeutic setting with your therapist.

   - I'm sorry, but this conversation is hard for me. Do you mind if we move on to something else?
   - This conversation is triggering a lot of my grief, and I need to take a break.
   - Thank you for asking about my loss, but I am not ready to talk about it.
   - I appreciate you acknowledging my loss, but I am not ready to talk about it.
   - _____

HOW TO ASK FOR HELP

The different parts of the *How to Ask for Help* worksheet are dedicated to supporting clients as they identify who can and cannot respond to their grief-related needs. This work will continue to help clients discover and distinguish their boundaries, which is so useful for grieving and anxiously grieving clients to regain and exercise control.

Clients often benefit from discussing this worksheet in session. With you as their guide and within a therapeutic setting, they may feel more comfortable experimenting with a variety of different responses. As with the other in-session activities, clients will benefit from further reflection on the process of asking for help.

As with the *How to Talk About Your Loss* worksheet, this worksheet has multiple sections:

1. Who Can Help You Grieve?

2. How Can They Help Me?

3. Who Can't Help Me Grieve?

4. Creating Boundaries for People Who Can't Help Me Grieve

HOW TO ASK FOR HELP

Asking for help can be difficult. This is the case for many people, even those who have not experienced loss. Though everyone in your corner will likely want the best for you, it is important to get the help you need— but only in the ways that you need and want it. Use this worksheet to discover the ways you can ask others for help.

1. **Who Can Help Me Grieve?**

   It is easier to ask for help when you feel supported by those in your support network. It's important to identify the people who are most capable of meeting your needs and whom you feel most comfortable asking for help.

   Make a list of some of the most helpful things people have said to you. Why were these words so helpful to you?

   - _____
   - _____
   - _____
   - _____
   - _____

   Make a list of the people in your life who are supportive presences in your grief journey. Identify how they've been supportive or why you are grateful for them.

Person	How Have They Been Supportive?
1.	
2.	
3.	
4.	
5.	

2. **How Can They Help Me?**

Make a list of the ways the people in your life can be helpful. Keep in mind that there are many ways that your family and friends can help you. I once had a client tell me that after her husband died, her best friend told her that every Tuesday she would show up on her porch with a meal. "I'll stay outside for ten minutes—if you want company, come out. If you don't, I'll just leave the meal." My client found this very comforting.

Check off the following ways other people can be of help to you:

☐ Drop off meals	☐ Help with transportation
☐ Have groceries delivered	☐ Help with research and planning
☐ Take out the trash	☐ Help with the funeral/memorial
☐ Take care of housecleaning	☐ Check on you daily/weekly
☐ Take care of pets	☐ Support you through a difficult anniversary
☐ Pick up prescriptions	

☐ _____

☐ _____

☐ _____

☐ _____

Now that you've identified the people who can help you, how they've supported you in the past, and how you would like to be supported now and in the future, identify a few ways you might be able to ask them for help or rely on them.

Person	How Can They Help You Now?
1.	
2.	
3.	
4.	
5.	

3. **Who Can't Help Me Grieve?**

Sometimes, you will want help from someone who is not able to offer it. This is common, but it can be especially hurtful after a loss. Make a list of some unhelpful or hurtful things people have said to you. Why were these words so unhelpful or hurtful?

- _____
- _____
- _____
- _____
- _____

4. **Creating Boundaries for People Who Can't Help Me Grieve**

There will be people and places that make you uncomfortable. You may feel uncomfortable sharing parts of your loss, your grief, or your grieving process with these people and these places.

Using the people you listed in the *Who Can't Help Me Grieve* section, make a list of any people or places that block or inhibit your grieving process. Next, using the boundary work you've already completed, write down safe boundaries you can use in your interactions with these people or in these places.

Person	Boundary I Can Establish
1.	
2.	
3.	
4.	
5.	

ACTIVITIES FOR ACTIVELY MANAGING AND COPING WITH GRIEF

Part of the aim of the previous activities is to help clients identify what their grief is like, what needs it poses, and who might be able to help them meet those needs. The following exercises can help clients to become more familiar with their different grief expressions. The familiarity can introduce clients to the changing nature of their grief, preparing them to be able to communicate the needs they have around their various grief expressions as they change.

JOURNAL PROMPTS FOR GRIEF

Grief journaling can be a powerful exercise, but it depends on the free expression of your clients' feelings. You can foster this by introducing clients to the concept of freewriting. With freewriting, clients write down all their thoughts and feelings in response to a particular prompt. While writing, they should not stop, reread, self-censor, or self-edit. Instruct them to keep their pen to paper and allow their thoughts to flow unimpeded.

Prepare clients for freewriting by reminding them that their journal is for themselves alone, that no one else will ever need to read what they've written, and that their journal is a safe place for them to express themselves. It can be useful to conduct a freewriting activity in session, wherein both you and the client engage in freewriting in response to the same prompt. Once clients express some comfort with the activity, you can give them a list of prompts and encourage them to integrate freewriting into their daily activities.

 JOURNAL PROMPTS

Pick a different journal prompt every day and freewrite your response. Remember that freewriting refers to writing quickly without censoring yourself, which includes stopping yourself from writing or editing what you've written. Try to keep your hands moving while you write, and don't pause to reread the lines you have just written. Don't cross anything out. Don't worry about spelling, punctuation, or grammar. Let yourself dive into the tough stuff, and don't avoid the scary stuff or the things you're afraid to say—this is sometimes where the best processing and healing takes place. Remember to be compassionate with yourself as you write. Use these examples to get you started:

- Today, I'm having a hard time with . . .
- Today, I am missing . . .
- The hardest time of day is . . .
- One thing I want to remember about my loved one is . . .
- A memory of my loved one that makes me laugh is . . .
- A memory with my loved one that makes me cry is . . .
- A comforting memory of my loved one is . . .

- I don't ever want to forget . . .
- My loved one's favorite holiday was . . .
- My loved one was most passionate about . . .
- My three favorite qualities of my loved one are . . .
- My loved one always used to say . . .
- I can honor my loved one by . . .
- I need more of . . .
- I need less of . . .
- I am angry about . . .
- I am most afraid of . . .
- I feel grief within my body in my . . .
- To be more compassionate toward myself today, I can . . .
- To be more compassionate with myself, I am willing to try . . .
- I feel most connected to my loved one when . . .
- One thing I wish I could do over with my loved one is . . .
- If I could forgive my loved one for something, it would be . . .
- If I could forgive myself for something, it would be . . .
- My favorite times with my loved one were . . .
- My most difficult times with my loved one were . . .
- My loved one always made me feel . . .
- When I am overwhelmed by grief, my mantra is . . .
- Something that makes me feel cared for is . . .
- One thing I wish my support system could understand is . . .
- One thing I wish my support system could help with is . . .
- I am ready to feel . . .

LETTER WRITING FOR GRIEF

I encourage letter writing for grief for the same reasons I encourage journal writing—and freewriting in particular: Sitting down to write, whether or not we have a recipient in mind, can have a freeing effect.

This is often the case when it comes to writing a letter because we can unburden ourselves in writing in ways we can't when we're talking to someone face-to-face. Maybe it's because when we write, we can express ourselves in an uninterrupted flow. Maybe it's because letters can be directed to a recipient without actually being sent to that recipient. Whatever the reason, writing letters to recipients, real and imagined, can be a powerful practice.

Discuss the possibility of letter writing with your client, providing them with the examples that follow. Remind them that these are not letters to be sent or shared, that they can say whatever they want or need to say in their letters, and that they don't have to share their words with anyone.

✉️ LETTER WRITING

Writing letters in the grief process is powerful. You can write them by hand or on a computer—to your loved one or anyone else you would like. Write as many as you need to. And remember that you don't have to share these letters with anyone. Here are some examples of letters you could write:

- Write a letter to the person who has died.
- Write a letter to yourself from your person.
- Write a letter to family or friends who are being supportive.
- Write a letter to family or friends who are not being supportive.
- Write a letter to your younger self.
- Write a letter to your future self.
- Write a letter of compassion for yourself.

MAKING SPACE FOR GRIEF

It's important for all grieving and anxiously grieving clients to designate space and time for grieving. Grieving people are often surprised to hear this. They may feel as though every moment of their day is already spent in some part of the grieving process. However, if you investigate this feeling further, you will frequently find that clients are spending their days protecting themselves from their grief expressions. Their grief feels so powerful and relentless that they often spend a lot of time distracting themselves from or otherwise avoiding active grief.

Because a client's ability to move through the grieving process is predicated on their ability to deeply feel all the expressions of their grief, you must support them in identifying the time and space for their expressions. This not only helps clients to manage the time they may be spending actively *not* feeling their grief, but it also helps ensure that their grief doesn't build up and spill over.

Encourage clients to identify where and when they will make space and time for their grief. This activity can be completed in session, in preparation for the grief plan described later in this chapter. Clients can also reflect on which of the previous activities felt most useful to them or if there are any other activities they might like to try.

IN-SESSION ACTIVITY

Let's consider the ways you can make space for grief. Think about your willingness and frequency for each of the following activities. Decide which ones resonate the most with you, and identify when and where you could integrate each into your day-to-day life:

- Journaling
- Meditation
- Yoga
- Therapy
- Grief groups
- Alone time to reflect and remember
- Time with others who share or understand your grief

AFFIRMATIONS FOR GRIEF

Whereas the previously mentioned activities will help clients as they take steps toward learning to cope with and manage their grief, affirmations for grief can offer soothing interventions in the here and now.

Affirmations are short, strong statements of positive, validating expressions. They are useful and convenient because they do not depend on context and can be used anywhere and at any time. They also do not rely on rationalization or explanation, which means they do not need to be accompanied by persuasion. Essentially, affirmations are simple statements of truth that clients can memorize and repeat to remind themselves of their own strengths, even in the midst of their grief and grief anxiety.

Introduce affirmations to grieving clients using the examples that follow. Then, work with clients to help them identify which affirmations resonate most with them, or they may be able to create an affirmation of their own. Allow clients to take the list of affirmations home with them to try out different phrases. Once they have identified their chosen affirmations, encourage them to practice saying the affirmations out loud in and out of session. Then, when clients struggle with grief or face challenges associated with their grief over the course of care, you can remind them of their affirmations.

 AFFIRMATIONS FOR CLIENTS

Repeat these affirmations whenever you are struggling with your grief:

- I accept all of my feelings and emotions.
- I can endure and survive this loss.
- I will take care of myself while I am grieving.
- My feelings matter and are important.
- My grief is normal.

- My grief will change with time.
- I can take as much time as I need to grieve.
- It's okay to fall apart.
- I am loved and supported.
- When I feel alone, I can reach out for support.
- I am doing the best I can.
- I accept myself in this moment.
- _____

MEDITATION SCRIPT FOR GRIEF

As discussed, all grieving clients benefit from beginning a meditation practice. And many of these clients will benefit further with extra guidance, especially as they begin a new practice. Integrating guided meditations into sessions helps provide this support. It can also familiarize clients with the rhythm of meditation as well as its numerous benefits.

Introduce the following meditation script to clients in session. Consider recording the session and offering clients the recording for their use at home or whenever they want to benefit from focusing in on their grief and allowing its expressions to move through them.

 MEDITATION SCRIPT FOR GRIEF

Find a comfortable place to sit or lie down. Close your eyes and begin to take slow, even breaths. Let any sounds fall away. Let any random thoughts just drift off. Simply focus on your breath and the sound of my voice.

[Pause]

Start by acknowledging all the grief and pain you are feeling. Notice how it feels in your body. Notice any thoughts that arise. It's okay to cry and it's okay not to cry too. Acknowledge that you are grieving and that you are hurting.

[Pause]

Continue breathing and letting yourself feel the grief moving through you. Remind yourself that you are safe and supported and that it's okay to be in your grief. Let any feelings and thoughts arise and then let them move through you, continuing to focus on the breath flowing in and out of your body.

[Pause]

Take a moment to feel kindness and compassion toward yourself at this time in your life. Feel compassion for all the grief you are experiencing, all the sadness you feel, all the hurt you are carrying. Try to see yourself as you would a child or a dear friend. What kind of love and kindness would you extend to them? Cultivate that same love and compassion for yourself. Let it wash over and through you. Let it comfort you.

[Pause]

Continue breathing and simply letting your grief exist. Remember that you are safe and that you are supported. You are grieving and that is okay. You are doing the very best you can at this time. You did not ask for this experience, but you are in it and you are okay.

[Pause]

Continue to feel that compassion for yourself. Remind yourself that you are supported in your grief. You are safe and you are loved and you are not alone. Imagine this feeling following you all the way through your day.

[Pause]

Slowly begin to deepen your breath and come back into your body. Take your time opening your eyes and returning to the room.

MY GRIEF PLAN

Clients cannot always plan for the emotions and feelings that arise in relationship to outer or internal stimuli. They can, however, plan for how they will handle their emotions and feelings. For grieving clients, a plan for grief will not control or necessarily moderate expressions of grief, but it will allow clients to feel in control of the ways that their grief impacts and affects them.

Creating an effective grief plan depends on clients' deep familiarity with their own grieving process, grieving expressions, and grief needs. Therefore, introduce clients to *My Grief Plan* after working in session on the therapeutic activities described earlier. Clients should be able to identify self-soothing strategies that they find effective, as well as be able to identify the most helpful individuals in their support network. They should be comfortable with affirmations and have worked to establish their own meditation practices. By consolidating the practices that bring them comfort into an accessible plan, clients gain a true sense of control over their grieving process, and this is often, in and of itself, a great comfort.

 CLIENT PLAN FOR GRIEF

Let's reflect on the all the strategies for grief you have experimented with over the course of our work together. Draw on this work to help you answer the following prompts as fully and specifically as possible:

- When I feel my grief, I will use these activities to soothe myself . . .
- When I feel my grief, I will call these people . . .
- When I feel my grief, I will use these affirmations . . .
- When I feel my grief, I will use this meditation . . .

REFLECTION

I've found that for many people, losing their loved one results in painful isolation and a sense they've been subsumed by grief. This chapter includes a wide variety of activities that encourage clients to externalize their grief and view it as an experience that is separate from who they are. These activities echo meditation: Completing them allows clients to gently focus on their experiences, emotions, feelings, behaviors, and physical symptoms and view them from a more neutral position. This frees them to identify the measures they can take to meet their needs and begin to soothe themselves, however their grief manifests.

CHAPTER 9

STRATEGIES FOR ANXIETY

Our anxiety does not come from thinking about
the future, but from wanting to control it.

—Kahlil Gibran

Although anxiety is a common reaction to loss, it's an underrecognized and underacknowledged part of the grieving process. When a client loses someone they love, it thrusts them into a new and uncertain world. They often feel alone and terribly vulnerable. They might also become suddenly and sharply aware of the world as an unpredictable and uncontrollable place. The symptoms of anxiety frequently arise as a response to some of these frightening realizations.

Though anxiety sometimes acts as a necessary response to danger, it does little to help clients manage or cope with their grief. Instead, it provokes a variety of other challenging emotions, feelings, behaviors, and physiological symptoms, including—for me—unpredictable panic attacks. When I was grieving the death of my mother, I wasn't able to focus on feeling the pain of my loss and allowing that pain to move through me. Instead, I was focused on trying to predict—so I could figure out how to avoid—acute bouts of panic.

Unmanaged grief anxiety can block important emotions and feelings associated with grief. It can divert a person's attention away from their loss and stall their grieving process. This is why it is sometimes understood as serving a protective function: Anxiety channels the intensity of grief into expressions that may seem easier or more straightforward to manage.

Yet anxiety in grief hinders a client's ability to heal. Expressions of anxiety don't take the place of more painful expressions of grief. In fact, expressions of anxiety are usually a sign that grief is being blocked, and if grief is blocked, it cannot be fully processed. When working with anxiously grieving clients, it's therefore vital to find ways to understand, reduce, and manage their anxiety so they can move through their grieving process more fluidly. You may feel that you're sometimes more focused on anxiety than grief in this work. However, you cannot help your clients grieve without responding to their anxiety.

In this chapter, I introduce a variety of activities for supporting clients with grief anxiety, including anxiety that manifests as intrusive or catastrophic thoughts and that which manifests as health anxiety. The activities will help you to guide your clients to safely explore their own anxiety as it manifests in their grieving process. Many of the activities should be introduced in session to guide clients toward identifying and managing their anxiety. Some activities can also be used as informal prompts and invitations to exploration and discussion. Clients may also benefit from completing some of these activities as homework, especially in the service of soliciting deeper reflections.

ACTIVITIES TO HELP CLIENTS IDENTIFY AND UNDERSTAND THEIR GRIEF ANXIETY

As we've learned in chapter 5, grieving clients who are also experiencing anxiety present in different ways. Some clients will have never experienced anxiety before, while others will see an uptick in their baseline anxiety levels. Some will experience old anxieties in unfamiliar ways, or they may experience a resurgence of familiar symptoms. Just as is the case with grief, helping your clients become familiar with the way their anxiety manifests is instrumental to working on, and through, their grieving process.

The activities that follow help clients identify and understand the emotions, feelings, behaviors, and physiological symptoms that may manifest as grief anxiety. Some clients may readily identify and understand their experience of grief anxiety, while others may benefit from supportive discussions to help establish the links between their loss and their grief anxiety. Similar to the approach to grief I described in the previous chapter, I find that when clients recognize their anxiety as a typical part of their grieving process, they often feel empowered to find strategies for coping with it.

ANXIETY INVENTORY

The *Anxiety Inventory* offers broad insight into your client's experience of anxiety. It is a useful addition to early sessions, particularly after supporting clients with activities for understanding and normalizing their grief from the previous chapters.

To conduct the inventory, use the *Anxiety Inventory* as the basis for an in-session discussion about anxiety. Then offer clients the worksheet for reflection outside of session. Depending on the client's previous experience with anxiety, the questions can also be used to educate them on anxiety and its relationship to grief.

Repeating the *Anxiety Inventory* in later sessions can also be useful. Repetition can help clients identify patterns in their anxiety, including potential triggers and effective coping mechanisms for specific emotions, feelings, behaviors, or symptoms. Repetition can also help clients to name the ways in which they are learning to manage their anxiety, and to seek support as they continue to process their loss.

ANXIETY INVENTORY

Rate the following statements on a scale of *never*, *sometimes*, *often*, or *all the time*.

I feel anxious, worried, or agitated.

☐ never   ☐ sometimes   ☐ often   ☐ all the time

I worry about one specific thing.

☐ never   ☐ sometimes   ☐ often   ☐ all the time

I worry about many different things.

☐ never   ☐ sometimes   ☐ often   ☐ all the time

My anxious thoughts are related to my loss.

☐ never   ☐ sometimes   ☐ often   ☐ all the time

I feel anxious for whole parts of a day.

☐ never   ☐ sometimes   ☐ often   ☐ all the time

I have trouble sleeping.

☐ never   ☐ sometimes   ☐ often   ☐ all the time

My appetite or eating habits change.

☐ never   ☐ sometimes   ☐ often   ☐ all the time

I feel anxious that something bad will happen.

☐ never   ☐ sometimes   ☐ often   ☐ all the time

I find it difficult to relax.

☐ never   ☐ sometimes   ☐ often   ☐ all the time

I find it difficult to manage my anxiety.

☐ never   ☐ sometimes   ☐ often   ☐ all the time

I share my anxiety with family and friends.

☐ never   ☐ sometimes   ☐ often   ☐ all the time

My anxiety affects my relationships.

☐ never   ☐ sometimes   ☐ often   ☐ all the time

My anxiety affects my work life.

☐ never   ☐ sometimes   ☐ often   ☐ all the time

My anxiety affects my daily functioning.

☐ never   ☐ sometimes   ☐ often   ☐ all the time

ANXIETY TRACKING JOURNAL

Although some clients will have had past encounters with anxiety, other clients will find that anxiety in general, or their particular experiences of anxiety subsequent to their loss, is something new and unfamiliar to them. Like me, they may experience their anxiety in the form of a panic attack or other obtrusive occurrence. They may not know what it is or where it came from. They may connect the experience to their physical health rather than to their grieving process.

A tracking journal can help clients begin to identify their anxiety expressions and become aware of the ways it manifests in their day-to-day lives. In this way, the journal acts as an aid to discovering connections between anxiety and grief. In fact, because it heightens client awareness of anxiety patterns, a tracking journal is a particularly helpful tool when used in tandem with other management and coping strategies. As clients become aware of their anxiety, they can learn to acknowledge and accept it as a part of their grieving process.

Introduce the *Anxiety Tracking Journal* in session. Then, send it home with clients, asking them to fill it out and bring it back to session for review and discussion.

ANXIETY TRACKING JOURNAL

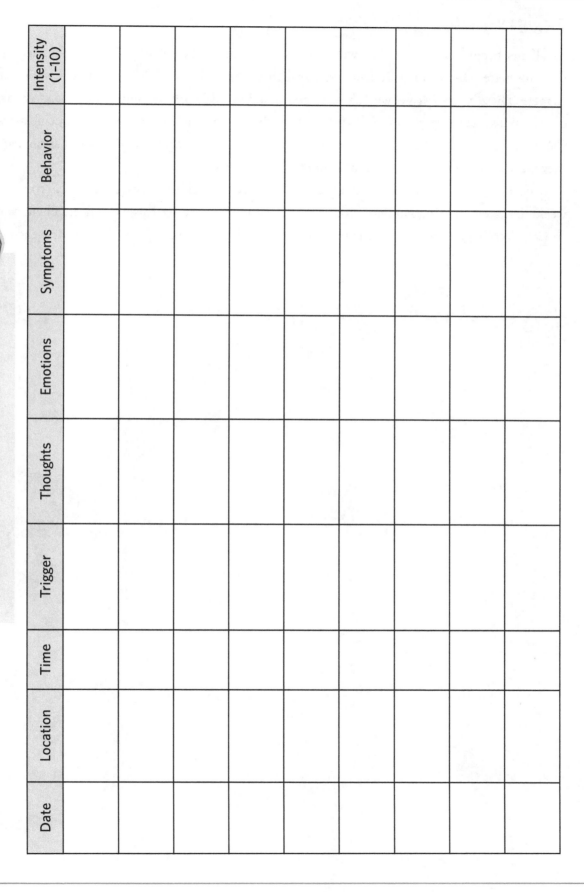

Date	Location	Time	Trigger	Thoughts	Emotions	Symptoms	Behavior	Intensity (1–10)

ANXIETY TRIGGERS

As clients become more familiar with their anxiety, they can begin to identify its triggers. When they are better able to identify triggers, they can better anticipate, and ultimately respond, to those triggers. The *Anxiety Triggers* worksheet acts as an aid to this work, helping clients discover the helpful coping skills that they already use and identify the contexts in which the skills are most useful. As clients recognize that they already use coping skills effectively, they often realize that anxiety doesn't inevitably lead to overwhelm. It can, with effort, be managed.

Accordingly, once clients have had an opportunity to track their anxiety over the course of a few weeks and are becoming familiar with its manifestations, introduce this worksheet. Then, as with the *Anxiety Tracking Journal*, ask clients to fill in the worksheet and bring it back for review each week.

ANXIETY TRIGGERS

List the common triggers that make you anxious and rate them on a scale of 1–10:

Social: _____

_____

Personal: _____

_____

Environmental: _____

_____

Other: _____

_____

Describe the symptoms you feel for each one:

Social: _____

_____

Personal: _____

_____

Environmental: _____

_____

Other: _____

_____

Describe the thoughts that come to mind for each one:

Social: _____

_____

Personal: _____

_____

Environmental: _____

_____

Other: _____

_____

What are some ways to avoid these triggers?

Social: _____

_____

Personal: _____

_____

Environmental: _____

_____

Other: _____

_____

When you can't avoid these triggers, how can you prepare to encounter them?

Social: _____

_____

Personal: _____

_____

Environmental: _____

_____

Other: _____

_____

Put a check mark by any coping skills you can use when you are triggered.

☐ Remove myself from the situation or environment

☐ Take a time out

☐ Use breathing exercises

☐ Meditate on _____

☐ Visualize _____

ACTIVITIES FOR MANAGING GRIEF ANXIETY

As clients begin to feel comfortable identifying and understanding their expressions of grief anxiety and the coping skills they already use, they generally feel more capable of considering active strategies for management. As with the active strategies for managing and coping with grief, these activities serve an empowering function. Your clients didn't have control over their loss, and they don't have control over their grief expressions. By identifying how they want to support themselves in their grief anxiety, however, they gain some control over their movement through the grieving process.

I AM IN CONTROL

The death of a loved one lays bare a client's lack of control over the universe. They couldn't save their loved one from death, no matter how badly they may have wanted to. This knowledge, for many, can be terrifying.

As clients explore their anxiety and connect it to their feelings of control, they can also begin to empower themselves with the *I Am in Control* worksheet. The worksheet supports clients as they identify the things in their life that they *can* control. Connecting this worksheet to the *Anxiety Tracking Journal* and the *Anxiety Triggers* worksheets offers clients comprehensive support as they work to identify their anxiety and begin to consider new responses they want to use to manage it.

Begin a discussion in session to help clients identify more and less realistic examples of things they can control. Then, ask clients to fill out the worksheet at home, bringing it back for reinforcement and further conversation.

I AM IN CONTROL

Use this worksheet to discover the things you do (and do not) have control over.

What things in my life do I have control over? (e.g., my boundaries, my actions, who I spend my time with)

_____

_____

_____

_____

_____

_____

_____

What things in my life do I have *no* control over? (e.g., the past, predicting what will happen, what other people think)

_____

_____

_____

_____

_____

_____

_____

_____

SELF-CHECK-IN

The *Self-Check-In* activity is a means to provide clients with ongoing support as they continue to identify what they can and cannot control. It is an ideal activity to complete at the beginning of each session. Regular completion offers opportunities to support and praise the client as they become better able to identify their feelings and more capable of finding effective coping and self-soothing strategies.

IN-SESSION ACTIVITY
Answer these questions each time you feel overwhelmed: • How am I feeling today? • What are three things that make me feel safe? • What are three things that make me feel capable? • What do I need to feel better?

NEW COPING SKILLS

As clients gain practice identifying the different ways their grief anxiety manifests and the aspects of their life that are and are not within their control, they can begin to brainstorm effective new coping strategies.

The *New Coping Skills* worksheet can be completed as homework, but clients typically benefit from therapist guidance in session. Call your clients' attention to connections they may not have noticed between what makes them feel anxious and how those feelings manifest in their body, thoughts, and actions. Remind clients of the coping strategies they already use and the actions they've identified as making them feel safe and capable.

During session, you and your clients can use the patterns they have already identified to brainstorm new coping skills with which they may want to experiment. The coping skills they identify on the *Anxiety Triggers* worksheet and *Self-Check-In* activity offer particular examples of coping from which clients may want to build off. When they have identified strategies for coping, ask them to experiment with their strategies and report back in future sessions.

NEW COPING SKILLS

Fill out this worksheet to create some new coping skills for when you feel anxious.

What are some things that make you feel anxious?

_____

_____

_____

_____

_____

_____

What do these anxious things make your body feel?

_____

_____

_____

_____

_____

_____

_____

What do these anxious things make you think?

_____

_____

_____

_____

_____

_____

_____

What do these anxious things make you do?

_____

_____

_____

_____

_____

When you feel anxious, you can cope by:

- ☐ Deep breathing
- ☐ Using positive self-talk
- ☐ Meditating
- ☐ Talking to a friend
- ☐ Going for a walk
- ☐ Writing in my journal
- ☐ Exercising
- ☐ _____
- ☐ _____
- ☐ _____

SOCIAL ANXIETY TRIGGERS

For a grieving individual, the hard-to-control variables that characterize most social situations can cause significant anxiety. In addition to stressors associated with the people involved or the event duration, grieving individuals may feel acutely alone. In the past, they may have navigated social situations with their loved one. Now that their person has died, they may be unsure how to relate to others.

To help clients prepare and mitigate anxiety associated with social situations, work with them on the *Social Anxiety Triggers* worksheet. This integrates elements of the *New Coping Skills* worksheet and prompts clients to create a list of the things they can control in almost any social situation, including identifying those things that make them feel more comfortable and those people whom they feel comfortable around. Taken together, their responses work toward a plan for handling social situations more comfortably.

As with many of the other activities and worksheets in this chapter, this worksheet should be introduced in session, where you can support clients as they explore both the challenges associated with social situations and the things about social situations that they can and cannot control. They can then take the questions home for further reflection and completion.

SOCIAL ANXIETY TRIGGERS

Use this worksheet to discover your social anxiety triggers and create a plan to work on them.

Describe the environments and situations that make you anxious.

_____

_____

_____

_____

List the anxious thoughts and beliefs that arise.

_____

_____

_____

_____

Describe the emotions you feel.

_____

_____

_____

_____

Describe the bodily sensations you experience.

_____

_____

_____

_____

Describe the behaviors that result.

_____

_____

_____

_____

Make a list of what helps you feel more comfortable.

_____

_____

_____

_____

Make a list of people you feel comfortable with.

_____

_____

_____

_____

Make a list of ways you can take care of yourself in these situations.

_____

_____

_____

_____

ACTIVITIES FOR MANAGING AND COPING WITH INTRUSIVE, CATASTROPHIC, AND NEGATIVE THOUGHTS

When a catastrophe occurs, it can be natural to begin to see the world through a catastrophic lens, constantly waiting for the other shoe to drop and expecting more bad things to happen. Many people experience this shift after the loss of their loved one. They may find that they encounter intrusive, catastrophic, and negative thoughts that they cannot and do not know how to control.

The following activities can help clients learn to harness these kinds of thoughts and find ways to diminish and cope with them. Revisit and repeat the *Intrusive Thoughts* and *De-Catastrophizing* activities as often as necessary in session, and consider asking clients to repeat them outside of session too. These not only act as a means for coping with painful intrusive and catastrophic thoughts, but they also help support your clients' efforts to externalize thought patterns and to modify their behavior toward self-care.

INTRUSIVE THOUGHTS

Intrusive thoughts are unwanted thoughts that appear in clients' minds, often without warning and repetitively. These thoughts are a very common part of the grieving process, but they are often unwelcome and can be distracting, disturbing, or distressing. Helping clients to consciously turn toward these thoughts and to create a plan to cope with them can help to free clients from their oppressiveness.

IN-SESSION ACTIVITY

You can learn to cope with intrusive thoughts by becoming aware of them, getting to know them, and developing an action plan for when you have them:

1. Describe the thought.
2. List the symptoms and behaviors that come with this thought.
3. Describe the way this thought is irrational.
4. Choose an activity to redirect away from the thought.
5. Choose a self-care technique.

DE-CATASTROPHIZING

When clients catastrophize, they exaggerate a problem and assume the worst possible outcome will come to pass. As with intrusive thoughts, catastrophic thoughts are a common form of grief anxiety. They often arise as a manifestation of health anxiety, and your clients may report that they cannot free themselves from fixating on worst-case scenarios. By supporting clients as they identify their worries and the potential consequences of their worries coming to pass, you help them begin to uncover their inherent resilience.

> ## IN-SESSION ACTIVITY
>
> You can learn to manage catastrophic thoughts with practice. Once you identify your thoughts, you can begin to question them and correct the distortions:
>
> - What are you worried about?
> - How likely is it that your worry will come true? Give examples of past experiences or evidence to support your answer.
> - If your worry does come true, what is the worst thing that could happen?
> - If your worry does come true, what is most likely to happen?
> - If your worry does come true, what are the chances you'll be okay?
>   - In one week _____%
>   - In one month ____ %
>   - In one year _____%

CHALLENGING NEGATIVE THOUGHTS

When clients grieve, they may find themselves overwhelmed by or otherwise fixated on negative thought patterns. They may repeatedly assume the worst about others, about themselves, or about their environments. Negative thoughts can be a coping mechanism: They help to set expectations as low as possible and to prepare for the worst.

However, negative thoughts are not typically realistic thoughts, and when clients are overwhelmed by negative thoughts, they are unable to feel or to process other important emotions associated with grief.

It can be difficult to break this pattern of negativity. In their initial efforts, some clients find that they are unable to consider neutral or positive outcomes. Yet, by repeating the prompts on the *Challenging Negative Thoughts* worksheet, clients can begin to practice reflecting on the utility of their negative thoughts, as well as on the relationship between their negative thoughts and external reality. Introduce the questions in session, and then ask them to use the worksheet out of session when they feel negative thoughts arise.

CHALLENGING NEGATIVE THOUGHTS

Whenever you find yourself having a negative thought, ask yourself the following questions.

What is your negative thought?

_____

_____

_____

_____

Is this thought helpful?

_____

_____

_____

_____

Is your thought based on facts or is it just your opinion? Explain.

_____

_____

_____

_____

What evidence do you have that what you are thinking is true?

_____

_____

_____

_____

What evidence do you have that your thought is false?

_____

_____

_____

_____

What other reason could explain why this is happening?

_____

_____

_____

_____

Are you jumping to conclusions? Explain.

_____

_____

_____

_____

If your thoughts come true, what is the worst thing that could happen?

_____

_____

_____

_____

If you thoughts come true, how can you cope?

_____

_____

_____

_____

POSITIVE SELF-TALK AND AFFIRMATIONS

Positive self-talk can be an antidote to negative, intrusive, or catastrophizing thoughts. In fact, affirmations can also help quell other forms of anxiety. By helping clients identify and articulate positive statements, you can help them begin to learn—or relearn, subsequent to their loss—to self-soothe. These are statements that bring grieving clients comfort and that they will feel comfortable repeating when their grief anxiety manifests. Use the following affirmations to help clients find positive statements that will work for them.

 AFFIRMATIONS FOR CLIENTS

Use this list of affirmations as the first step in identifying specific positive self-talk that will work for you when you feel anxious or experience unwelcome thoughts:

- It's okay not to feel okay.
- This feeling won't last forever.
- These are just feelings and they will go away.
- I have dealt with hard things before.
- I can do hard things.
- This situation will make me stronger.
- These are just thoughts, not facts.
- I can change my thoughts whenever I want to.
- I am safe.
- I am supported.
- I am loved.
- I can handle my emotions.
- _____

ACTIVITIES FOR IDENTIFYING AND MANAGING HEALTH ANXIETY

Health anxiety is another common anxiety that presents after loss. For clients who experience it, health anxiety is typically characterized by obsessive and irrational worry that they may become seriously ill or have a serious medical condition. Even clients who have lost a loved one to something other than illness, such as an accident or suicide, will frequently develop health anxiety.

Health anxiety can take many forms. Generally, clients experience an extreme preoccupation with somatic symptoms, such as pain or fatigue, which then causes major emotional distress and problems with functioning. Clients may obsessively worry about these symptoms and frequently seek medical care, and some will continue to search for an explanation for their somatic symptoms even when serious conditions have been ruled out. Or, adversely, they may avoid medical care at all costs, afraid of what they might find out.

The following activities are designed to help clients identify and understand their health anxiety and cope with, as well as diminish, associated anxious thoughts. As with most forms of grief anxiety, health anxiety often manifests as a partial response to the fears associated with a lack of control. Clients may experience health anxiety in conjunction with catastrophic and negative thoughts. They may feel that they are not in control of every aspect of their bodies, and they may need urgent reassurance that their bodies and functioning are unimpaired. The activities in this section can help clients shift their focus from their health anxiety to other areas of their life. The activities also aim to empower clients to identify and reflect on the things about their health and their functioning that they can control.

HEALTH ANXIETY INVENTORY

The *Health Anxiety Inventory* offers broad insight into a client's experience of expressions of health anxiety and invites a valuable discussion in early sessions. This worksheet is a helpful exercise to repeat over the course of care—in or out of session—to gauge the differences in clients' experiences.

HEALTH ANXIETY INVENTORY

Answer the following questions, providing as much detail as possible, to gain a broad picture of your anxiety surrounding your health.

When do you experience anxiety about your health?

_____

_____

_____

What are your anxious thoughts about illness and health?

_____

_____

_____

Are there specific experiences that contribute to your anxiety about your health?

_____

_____

_____

Do you worry about specific illnesses?

_____

_____

_____

Do you seek information and reassurance about your health?

_____

_____

_____

Do you notice and zoom in on physical sensations in your body?

_____

_____

_____

Do you misinterpret physical sensations in your body?

_____

_____

_____

Do you check your body and your health frequently?

_____

_____

_____

Do you check symptoms and self-diagnose online?

_____

_____

_____

Do you avoid situations in which you might get sick or contract an illness?

_____

_____

_____

Do you feel uncomfortable with or avoid medical care?

_____

_____

Do you frequently seek out medical care?

_____

_____

_____

Do you worry about your loved ones getting sick?

_____

_____

_____

Do you worry about what will happen if you get sick?

_____

_____

_____

What do you feel when you get anxious about your health?

_____

_____

_____

How do you behave when you get anxious about your health?

_____

_____

_____

What coping strategies can you use when you feel anxiety about your health?

_____

_____

_____

Who can you talk to about your fears regarding your health?

_____

_____

_____

HEALTH ANXIETY TRACKING JOURNAL

Clients encounter health anxiety in a number of ways. Some may feel that they are negatively fixated on their health. Others may feel that although they are fixated on their health, their behavior is not problematic or is not an expression of anxiety. Still others may be caught up in their health anxiety and not yet able to view it as a discernible pattern.

For clients who express anxiety about their health (whether or not they identify their anxiety as a source of discomfort), the tracking journal can help. The journal can encourage clients to become aware of the different ways their health anxiety manifests daily. Alongside the activities for managing and coping, the journal heightens client awareness and enables their intervention. Send the tracking template home with clients, and then review it in session each week.

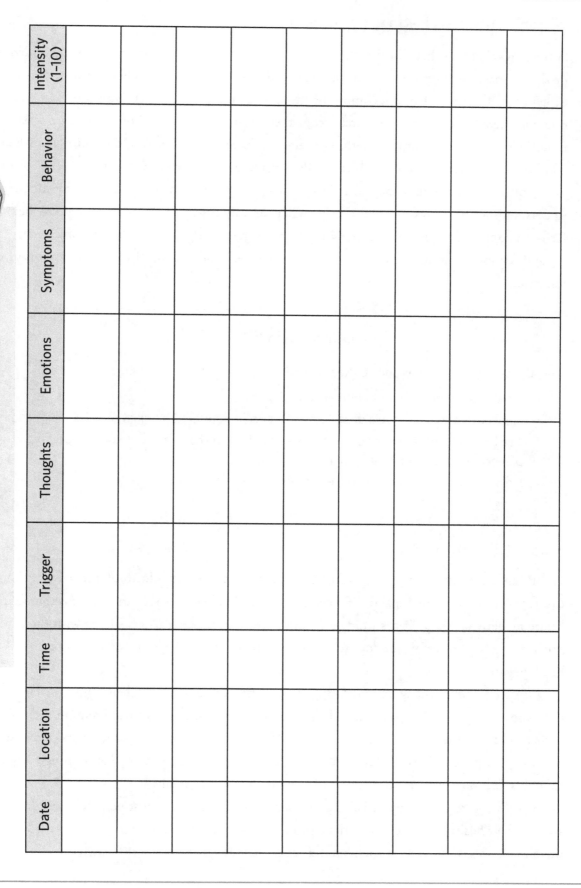

HEALTH ANXIETY TRACKING JOURNAL

Date	Location	Time	Trigger	Thoughts	Emotions	Symptoms	Behavior	Intensity (1–10)

WHERE DID MY HEALTH WORRIES ORIGINATE?

Supporting clients as they discover the origins of their health anxiety can encourage their identification of the connections between this anxiety and their grieving process. When opening this discussion, explain that health anxiety is a common and natural expression of grief. Point out that when a loved one dies, people can't help but to reflect on their own health and wellness. In some cases, however, these reflections can become something more like fixation. Ruminating on symptoms when serious conditions have been ruled out can cause distress and even disturb functioning.

Explain to clients that they can shift their focus away from health anxiety by identifying and understanding the origins of their health anxiety and by engaging in activities that can help them to face and cope with their fears. Although you can introduce this topic in session, ask clients to reflect on and complete the following questions outside of session. Then, discuss their responses together in session.

 QUESTIONS FOR CLIENTS

Let's identify your experience of health anxiety:

- How and when did your health anxiety begin?
- How has your loved one's death played a part in your health anxiety?
- Are there any other experiences you can think of, perhaps from the past, that have played a part in your health anxiety?
- How do these experiences make you feel about your health?

FACING YOUR FEARS

Health anxiety very often provokes fear because it touches on the death of a loved one. Sometimes, this fear can be very intense and can keep grieving individuals stuck in the patterns that sustain their health anxiety. Helping clients to identify and acknowledge the fears associated with their health and functioning is a powerful step toward supporting them as they begin to move through their fear and break negative patterns.

Of course, acknowledging and facing their fears is almost always challenging for clients, even if they know that doing so is ultimately helpful. It is important to continually remind them that facing their fears helps them to manage those fears: When they actively try *not* to think about something scary, it usually doesn't work. They will not only end up spending their time pushing away the scary thoughts, but they also give those fears even more power and intensity.

The *Facing Your Fears* worksheet can help clients address their most persistent and intrusive fears around their health. Consequently, these prompts may activate some clients, so introduce and discuss them in session, and then ask clients to reflect outside of session and write down their answers.

FACING YOUR FEARS

Write about your biggest health fear in as much detail as possible. Write about what it would be like to live through that fear. Include as many details, facts, thoughts, and feelings, as possible. This exercise is meant to be uncomfortable, so if breaks are needed, please take them.

After you have written your story, read it multiple times until it begins to lose its heat and energy. You can expect intense emotions to surface as you read it, but remind yourself that you can tolerate these emotions. Doing this will enable you to experience these fearful thoughts with less distress.

SCHEDULING TIME TO WORRY

Health anxiety can be all-consuming: When everyday aches and pains are considered evidence of disease, it's difficult to ignore that pain and move on, even if the pain is seemingly small and insignificant. The *Scheduling Time to Worry* activity encourages clients to put a time limit on their worries. It can help them consolidate fears—fears that might otherwise take over their entire day—into one block of time. It can also help clients realize that they have more control over their worries and fears than they might think.

Clients may experience this activity as somewhat counterintuitive. If this is the case, it can be helpful to explain that scheduling time to worry works to proactively manage anxious thoughts and prevent those thoughts from taking over hours and days. Once they've chosen a designated worry time, clients can begin to push back against the anxious thoughts that arise outside that time. They may choose to integrate positive self-talk into their reminder of their designated worry time. This can help turn anxious thoughts into a prompt for affirmation.

IN-SESSION ACTIVITY

Let's schedule your own worry time:

- My worry time is scheduled for . . .
- Whenever anxious thoughts come up outside of my worry time, I will tell myself . . .

CHANGING MY HEALTH BELIEFS

For some clients, their health anxiety may feel hard to manage or to cope with because it's fueled by core beliefs. Whether positive or negative, core beliefs are powerful motivating sources that sustain some of the most persistent thought patterns. When grieving clients experience sustained health anxiety, it is important to lead them in investigating their core beliefs. Once clients are able to identify and articulate their core beliefs, they can then reflect on those beliefs and potentially change them.

The *Changing My Health Beliefs* worksheet helps clients to identify their core beliefs. Begin this discussion in session by defining the concept of core beliefs and including examples. For instance, someone may believe they will get cancer just like their loved one. Another person may think if they get cancer, they will certainly die from it. Still another may believe that if they don't constantly check their body, it will be too late by the time an illness presents itself. A client's core beliefs may be painful or upsetting for them to discover and hear, particularly if they haven't ever considered the beliefs that sustain their fears. Once you have worked through any feelings of upset, initiate a deeper discussion to challenge these beliefs. Ask the client to continue reflecting on their beliefs and to revisit their answers to the questions outside of session.

CHANGING MY HEALTH BELIEFS

Identifying the core beliefs that support your views about your health can uncover important connections to your experiences of health anxiety. Answer the questions below to identify core beliefs that may benefit from revision.

What are your core beliefs? (e.g., "I believe if I get cancer, I will die," "If I don't constantly check my body, it will be too late by the time an illness presents itself")

_____

_____

_____

_____

What evidence do you have that this belief is true? What evidence do you have that it is not true?

_____

_____

_____

_____

Is there an alternative belief that could also be true?

_____

_____

_____

_____

Are you ignoring or dismissing evidence that contradicts this belief?

_____

_____

_____

_____

Can you identify any distortions within this belief?

_____

_____

_____

_____

What would you say to a friend who had this belief?

_____

_____

_____

_____

How can you rephrase a new, realistic core belief?

_____

_____

_____

_____

DEATH ANXIETY

While core beliefs may motivate health anxiety, expressions of health anxiety often lightly mask death anxiety. As clients gain some comfort with identifying and understanding their anxiety, connecting its expressions to their experiences, and identifying ways to cope with it and manage it, they will likely be more prepared to discuss their fears of death.

In the spirit of uncovering fears so that they do not grow larger in the shadows, help clients illuminate their specific fears of death with the *Death Anxiety* worksheet. Prepare clients for the discussion of death anxiety by explaining the connection between health anxiety and death anxiety. Then, give them the worksheet to fill in outside of session. Their answers can help guide further reflective discussion about their fear of death and can inform the following *My Anxiety Plan* activity.

DEATH ANXIETY

Answer these questions, providing as much detail as possible, to identify and better understand your anxiety around death.

When do you experience anxiety about death?

_____

_____

_____

What are your anxious thoughts about death?

_____

_____

_____

Are there specific experiences that contribute to your anxiety about death?

_____

_____

_____

Do you worry about the physicality of death (i.e., potential pain and suffering)?

_____

_____

_____

Do you worry what will happen to your loved ones after you die?

_____

_____

_____

Do you worry about what happens after death?

_____

_____

_____

What do you feel when you get anxious about death?

_____

_____

_____

How do you behave when you get anxious about death?

_____

_____

_____

Who can you talk to about your fears around death?

_____

_____

_____

What coping strategies can you use when you feel anxiety about death?

_____

_____

_____

MY ANXIETY PLAN

My Anxiety Plan offers an efficient guide to the tools for responding to expressions of anxiety. As with so many other elements in grief work, no plan, no matter how comprehensive, can take away the pain, frustration, anger, anxiety, and other feelings that will arise over the course of the grieving process. However, this plan, like *My Grief Plan* from chapter 8, stands as a testament to the work your clients have done to identify their expressions of anxiety, to feel their expressions of anxiety, and to cope with and manage their expressions of anxiety. The plan is evidence of their ability to exercise their power, even when they feel like they have been made radically vulnerable by their grief.

 CLIENT PLAN FOR ANXIETY

Let's reflect on the all the strategies for anxiety you have experimented with over the course of our work together. Draw on this work to help you answer the following prompts as fully and specifically as possible:

- When I feel anxious, I will use these activities to soothe myself . . .
- When I feel anxious, I will call these people . . .
- When I feel anxious, I will use these affirmations . . .
- When I feel anxious, I will use this mindfulness technique . . .
- When I feel anxious, I will use this meditation . . .

REFLECTION

Anxiety is a common experience to loss. Yet, it is not always a point of focus in grief work. The activities in this chapter help respond to this disjunction. They encourage clients to look more closely at their anxiety and to understand what emotions and feelings their anxiety might be blocking or inadvertently hiding. By learning to identify and name their anxiety and to manage its various expressions, grieving clients can begin to feel more comfortable when other painful, difficult, and complicated emotions and feelings arise.

CHAPTER 10

STRATEGIES FOR ANGER

I sat with my anger long enough, until she told me her real name was grief.

—Isaac Rowe

nger, as I described in chapters 3 and 4, is such a common emotion of grief that it has been enshrined in Elisabeth Kübler-Ross's five stages of grief. It's an expression of frustration, and there are many reasons to feel frustrated after a loss. However, like anxiety and so many other expressions of grief, anger is also a reaction to a loss of control.

Clients may feel angry after a loss because they suddenly realize, consciously or not, that they have much less control over the world than they may have thought. They may feel frustrated and angry that this loss of control extends to their seemingly ungovernable thoughts, emotions, feelings, and behaviors.

They may also feel angry at specific situations and specific people. They may even be angry at their loved one who has died. They might be angry at themselves or at family members, perhaps for not stopping their loved one from dying. They might be angry at friends, at clergy, or at medical personnel. When you work with clients who are experiencing anger, you might even think they are angry at you and your inability to take away their pain, anger, and frustration.

While anger is in some ways healthy, it can also be toxic. It's a powerful emotion, and as such, it exerts a strong gravitational pull, especially for people who find it easier to feel anger than to feel the more tender and vulnerable emotions that anger may shield. Whatever variations of anger a grieving person is experiencing, it's important to the grieving process to help them identify it, feel it, explore it, and eventually release it.

In this chapter, I introduce a variety of activities for helping clients to work with and through anger. The activities can be used in session to support clients as they learn strategies for identifying and managing their anger. They can also be used during sessions as informal prompts and invitations to foster progressively deeper exploration. Clients will also benefit from completing some of these activities as worksheets outside of session. However you choose to use them, the activities can help clients safely explore—and learn to manage and cope with—their own anger as it manifests throughout their grieving process.

ACTIVITIES TO HELP CLIENTS IDENTIFY AND UNDERSTAND THEIR ANGER

Anger can be healthy, but it can also be unhealthy. Anger that is directed outward, that is the most dominant emotion experienced by a person, that feels out of control or is a source of regret, or that arises out of proportion to the provocation can indicate the kind of anger that is veering into unhealthy territory. Although it isn't possible to simply make this anger go away, it can typically be managed.

For most clients, constructively expressing and releasing anger requires identifying the anger when it occurs and understanding its provocations and sources. This is not always easy, and when a client's anger is complicated by grief, it is exponentially more difficult.

The anger your clients may feel after the death of their person can be multifaceted and can point in many directions. A grieving person may be angry at the world, at death, or at god. They may be furious at loved ones, including the person who has died, and at themselves, They may sense that their anger serves a protective function, and they may consequently avoid identifying it or be otherwise reluctant to discuss it. They may also already sense that their anger can't be speedily discharged with an apology or an admission of wrongdoing, whether their own or another's.

Consequently, it's often necessary to work with clients to identify their anger before asking them to inventory and track it. An exploratory discussion can help to destigmatize the anger clients may feel. Although it's a common emotion associated with grief, anger can provoke shame. Clients may feel that their anger is out of control, so they work hard to repress it. Clients may feel that their anger is so toxic that it can't be expressed. Clients may simply feel that their anger doesn't make sense as a response to loss. Regardless, they will likely benefit from an educative, exploratory discussion that prepares them for the activities in this chapter.

IDENTIFYING ANGER

To help your clients constructively express and release anger, you first need to help them identify their anger and its manifestations. This will open the door to understanding what other feelings their anger might be hiding. Only after the client has identified and fully understood its function as a shield, will anger management and coping mechanisms be effective.

To work on anger with your grieving clients, discuss the signs and symptoms of anger to open a conversation about their own anger and associated expressions.

Signs of Unhealthy Anger

As I've discussed, a healthy amount of anger is reasonable when a client is grieving. However, when anger overtakes their feelings as the primary emotion, it may become detrimental or unhealthy. The following are some of the most common signs of unhealthy anger:

- Hurting others either verbally or physically
- Constantly feeling angry

- Feeling that your anger is out of control

- Frequently regretting something you said or did when angry

- Noticing that small, petty, or seemingly insignificant things make you angry

In addition to outward expressions, anger manifests in a variety of physical symptoms. Many people already know that that they clench their jaws or their fists when they are angry, or that they feel a tightness in their chest when they are provoked. However, anger also manifests in less recognizable physical symptoms.

Physical Symptoms of Anger

Discuss the physical symptoms of anger with clients to help them identify their own symptoms and relate them to their experience. This will prepare clients to complete the anger inventory in the next section.

- Churning feelings in your stomach

- Tightness in your chest

- An increased and rapid heartbeat

- Weakening in legs

- Muscles that tense up

- Sweating palms

- A sudden feeling of warmth or sweatiness

- A sudden urge to go to the toilet

ANGER INVENTORY

The *Anger Inventory* offers broad insight into a client's experience of anger. As with the *Grief Inventory* and the *Anxiety Inventory*, this inventory is a useful addition to grief work and helps you and the client to gain a broad understanding of how, how often, and how intensely their anger manifests.

To conduct the inventory, give clients a handout of the following questions and ask them to rate each one. If they have difficulty identifying or recognizing their anger, the questions can be used as the basis for a more dynamic in-session discussion of anger. Depending on their experience with anger in the context of grieving, the questions can also be used to provide a deeper education on the relationship between anger and grief.

As with the other inventories, repeating the *Anger Inventory* in later sessions can be useful for helping clients in identifying patterns in their anger, including potential triggers and effective coping mechanisms for specific emotions, feelings, behaviors, or symptoms. Repetition can also help clients name the ways in which they are learning to manage their anger, and to seek support as they continue to process their loss.

ANGER INVENTORY

Put a check mark by the following statements that describe your relationship with anger.

- ☐ I feel angry sometimes.
- ☐ I feel angry most of the time.
- ☐ I feel angry all the time.
- ☐ I am angry that my person died.
- ☐ I feel angry about the way my person died.
- ☐ I feel angry at one person.
- ☐ I feel angry at multiple people.
- ☐ I feel angry at myself.
- ☐ I feel angry when I think about the past.
- ☐ I feel angry when I think about my present circumstances.
- ☐ I feel angry when I think about the future.
- ☐ I don't know what to do about my anger.
- ☐ I have coping tools I use for my anger.
- ☐ I will always be angry.
- ☐ I know I will only be angry for a little while.
- ☐ My anger causes me to make poor decisions.
- ☐ My anger distracts me from tasks and regular functioning.
- ☐ My anger keeps me up at night.
- ☐ My anger makes me tired.
- ☐ My anger interferes with my work.
- ☐ My anger interferes with my social life.
- ☐ My anger interferes with my relationships.
- ☐ My anger makes me shout.
- ☐ My anger scares people.
- ☐ No one knows how angry I feel.
- ☐ Some people know how angry I feel.
- ☐ Everyone knows how angry I feel.
- ☐ I feel so angry I want to hurt someone.
- ☐ I want to stop feeling angry.
- ☐ I never want to stop feeling angry.

ANGER TRACKING JOURNAL

For some clients, anger in general, or their particular expressions of anger subsequent to their loss, may feel strange and unfamiliar. They may experience frustration and rage in ways they've never experienced before. Or they may express annoyance and irritation in response to situations that didn't used to bother them or that don't seem commensurate with their response. Depending on their cultural or family background, some clients may also be unable or unwilling to fully acknowledge their anger.

A tracking journal can help clients become aware of all the ways their anger may manifest in their day-to-day lives. As with the *Anxiety Tracking Journal*, this activity is a useful tool for clients to get know their anger. It makes clients aware of their anger so they can begin to acknowledge and accept anger as it manifests in their grieving process. Send the journal template home with clients and then review it in session each week.

ANGER TRACKING JOURNAL

Date	Location	Time	Trigger	Thoughts	Emotions	Symptoms	Behavior	Intensity (1-10)

ANGER TRIGGERS

Once clients have had an opportunity to track their anger over the course of a few weeks, introduce the *Anger Triggers* worksheet. When they become more familiar with their triggers, they will be better able to anticipate and respond to those triggers. This worksheet also encourages clients to discover their intuitive coping skills and to identify which of these skills are helpful and in which contexts. The identification can show clients that their anger doesn't have to be suppressed, nor must it inevitably mount. With effort, their anger can be proactively managed.

As with the *Anger Tracking Journal*, begin the discussion surrounding this worksheet in session. Then, ask clients to fill it in and bring it back for review in session each week.

ANGER TRIGGERS

List the common triggers that make you angry and rate them on a scale of 1–10:

Social: _____

_____

Personal: _____

_____

Environmental: _____

_____

Other: _____

_____

Describe the symptoms you feel for each one.

Social: _____

_____

Personal: _____

_____

Environmental: _____

_____

Other: _____

_____

Describe the thoughts that come to mind for each one:

Social: _____

_____

Personal: _____

_____

Environmental: _____

_____

Other: _____

_____

What are some ways to avoid these triggers?

Social: _____

_____

Personal: _____

_____

Environmental: _____

_____

Other: _____

_____

When you can't avoid these triggers, how can you prepare to encounter them?

Social: _____

_____

Personal: _____

_____

Environmental: _____

_____

Other: _____

_____

Put a check mark by any coping skills you can use when you are triggered.

☐ Remove myself from the situation or environment

☐ Take a time out

☐ Use breathing exercises

☐ Meditate on _____

☐ Visualize _____

JOURNAL PROMPTS FOR ANGER

The following prompts help clients go deeper into their answers from the *Anger Tracking Journal* and *Anger Triggers* to better understand their anger and to locate its sources. Anger is not an emotion that ever really disappears, but as your clients learn more about their anger, including what they like and dislike about it, they can learn how to more constructively react to anger when it arises.

Remind clients that freewriting in their journal is for their eyes only. It is a safe place that they can write anything they need to express. Give them some prompts, such as the following examples, and encourage them to integrate freewriting into their daily activities.

 JOURNAL PROMPTS

Use the prompts that speak to you to begin to identify, acknowledge, and fully feel your anger:

- I am angry because . . .
- If my anger could speak, it would say . . .
- My anger makes me feel . . .
- My anger hurts me because . . .
- My anger helps me because . . .
- The person who makes me the most angry is . . .
- I am angry at myself because . . .
- I am angry at God because . . .
- When I am angry, it is really because . . .
- In my body my anger feels like . . .
- If my anger was a color, it would be . . .
- I enjoy feeling angry when . . .
- I regret feeling angry when . . .
- One time my anger got me into trouble was . . .
- What calms me down when I am angry is . . .
- The tools I can use when I am angry are . . .
- If I didn't feel angry today, I would . . .
- One way I have used my anger constructively was . . .
- Three things that distract me from feeling angry are . . .
- I know I'm getting better at managing my anger because . . .

UNDERNEATH ANGER: WHAT ELSE ARE YOU FEELING?

Anger is powerful and can give clients strength when they feel like they need it. However, anger often covers up other difficult emotions, especially sadness and fear. For grieving clients, anger often protects them from feeling anguished and exposed.

To continue helping clients move through their anger, it will likely be necessary to support them as they work to understand all the other emotions that they're feeling underneath their anger. Once clients have had a chance to identify and express their anger using the other activities in this section, introduce the *Underneath Anger* worksheet to help clients identify what else they're feeling as they grieve.

UNDERNEATH ANGER

Use this worksheet to explore any underlying emotions beneath your anger.

1. I am angry about _____

   _____

   This makes me sad because _____

   _____

   This makes me scared because _____

   _____

2. I am angry about _____

   _____

   This makes me sad because _____

   _____

   This makes me scared because _____

   _____

3. I am angry about _____

   _____

   This makes me sad because _____

   _____

   This makes me scared because _____

   _____

ACTIVITIES TO HELP CLIENTS MANAGE AND COPE WITH ANGER

The activities in the preceding section help clients get to know their anger and its many sources. The activities in this section are designed to help clients to manage, express, release, and generally cope with their anger, and the other emotions their anger might be hiding, as it continues to manifest in their grieving process.

Many people will experience anger, rage, frustration, fury, and intense irritation or annoyance for a long time after the loss of their person. For some, angry emotions will come and go. For others, angry emotions may be a stronger, more difficult to manage, or more lasting part of their grief.

Revisit and repeat the activities as often as necessary in session, and ask clients to repeat activities outside of session as well. Practice and repetition will encourage clients to work toward modifying their anger in beneficial, healing ways.

ANGER MANAGEMENT TECHNIQUES

Introduce the following techniques to manage anger with clients and encourage them to review the techniques regularly. Doing so will ensure that when anger arises, they will have ready access to a variety of tools for anger management.

ANGER MANAGEMENT TECHNIQUES

Recognize anger early:
- Look for warning signs like yelling, arguing, feeling hot, balling fists, or shaking.
- Recognize when triggers arise, and stay aware of how your emotions rise.

Take a timeout:
- When you feel yourself growing angry, remove yourself from the situation or environment.
- If other people are involved, let them know you need to take some time away.
- Remember that problems aren't solved when one or more people are angry.

Breathe deeply:
- Take time to breathe.
- Use any type of breathing exercise that works for you.
- Take at least 5–10 minutes to breathe calmly and deeply before reassessing your anger level.

Safely express your anger:
- Journal about your anger.
- Talk to a friend or therapist about what you are feeling.
- Write a letter.

Use healthy outlets:
- Throw or break something safely.
- Tear up paper.
- Go outside and throw rocks in a pond.
- Stomp on the ground.
- Break up or hit empty cardboard boxes.
- Scream in private or into a pillow.
- Sing at the top of your lungs.

Consider the consequences:
- What will be the outcome of your anger-fueled action?
- Will arguing help?
- Will you be happier after acting out?

Release anger with exercise:
- Exercise is a form of emotional release.
- Exercise releases calming hormones and chemicals.
- Try cardio like running or swimming.
- Dance to loud music.

Release anger with visualization:
- Visualize a calm place.
- Visualize feeling peaceful.
- Visualize releasing your anger.

LETTER WRITING FOR ANGER

Anger is often a challenging emotion for grieving clients to process, especially if the anger is directed at a person or an event who did not purposefully incite ire. As mentioned earlier, it is even common for a grieving person to be angry at their loved one who has died. This anger is often painful, and it is very difficult to express. Outside of a therapeutic setting, it is an anger that can bewilder others, making it hard for them to listen to or understand a grieving person's feelings. This is yet another reason why grieving people may strive to suppress and repress anger.

Although many forms of anger after grief may not seem rational, they make sense. When a client's person dies, they might feel intolerable frustration that the death has occurred and that their loved one is no longer with them. This frustration is a response to the stress of death, but it's a big, diffuse emotion. In fact, because it's such a big emotion, it can feel much more accessible than other emotions. Clients may find that it's easier to express anger, even if their anger is harder to direct or to otherwise manage.

Writing—and letter writing in particular—offers an opportunity for a more complete expression of anger, especially anger that may seem irrational. Encouraging a grieving client to write to the person or entity to whom they are angriest can allow them to express or vent the roiling emotions they feel inside, smoothing the way for further release. This letter is not for sending, so clients can write what they need to write, to anyone or anything, without worrying about hurting the recipient.

 LETTER WRITING

Writing letters when you're angry is a healthy way to express your anger. These do not have to be letters you send—they can be just for you. Write them in a journal or on a computer. Tell the person or the entity why you are angry, and describe your feelings. Try writing letters to:

- The person you lost
- Family members
- Friends
- Medical personnel
- Coworkers
- God
- Yourself
- Your anger itself

DEEP BREATHING FOR ANGER

Deep breathing is a versatile tool that helps to calm and soothe most people. You have already learned that deep breathing is a strategy for anxiety, but it is also incredibly effective for irruptions of anger—in fact, it is a great tactic for slowing down feelings of all kinds.

When we get angry, our central nervous system becomes dysregulated, and we find that we start to feel out of control. Maybe we start to exhibit physical symptoms, such as a rapid heartbeat, sweaty palms, or a tightness in our chest. Or maybe we lash out in unhealthy ways that we regret.

Deep breathing is critical for to help clients instill a sense of calm and regulate their central nervous system. However, to rely on deep breathing during an angry episode, clients must already be comfortable with deep breathing techniques. To support them with this, discuss deep breathing's role in managing anger, and practice breathing deeply in every session. Then, encourage your clients to practice deep breathing on their own throughout their day.

IN-SESSION ACTIVITY

Practice deep breathing according to these instructions as often as possible:

1. Find a comfortable place to sit or lie down.
2. Close your eyes.
3. Begin by breathing in deeply through your nostrils and filling your belly.
4. Now start to breathe in through your nostrils for three counts.
5. Then, hold your breath for nine counts.
6. Finally, breathe out slowly for six counts.
7. Repeat this cycle 5-10 times.

RELEASING ANGER

Sometimes, clients recognizing their anger, finding a constructive outlet for it, or breathing through it is not enough. They may be unable to move on until they explicitly release their anger. This is particularly the case when anger is complicated by other variables. To support your grieving clients who need to release their anger, use your time together in session to introduce the following step-by-step strategy. Then, ask the clients to complete the steps on their own on a regular basis to get into the practice of releasing their anger.

IN-SESSION ACTIVITY

Use the following steps when you feel angry:

- Recognize and acknowledge the anger.
- Examine the underlying emotions (e.g., fear and pain).
- Examine the reason for being angry. Is it justified? Is it rational?

- Ask yourself what you are getting out of being angry.
- Ask yourself what your anger is costing you.
- Consider forgiveness.
- Commit to releasing your anger.
- Visualize yourself at peace.

DECIDING TO FORGIVE

For grieving people, anger is not always the consequence of feeling frustrated or vulnerably out of control after the death of a loved one. Sometimes, anger is the result of a breach in a relationship. A client may feel wronged by real or perceived mistakes and be angry as a response.

Although forgiveness may be the only tool that can repair this breach, forgiveness is not always easy to give or to receive. This may be especially the case for a grieving client, for whom the anger they feel toward the person who has wronged them is tied up in the anger associated with their loved one's death.

To support your clients in exploring the issue of forgiveness as it relates to their anger, discuss the following questions together. Depending on the discussion, you might encourage clients to journal their answers outside of session, or to use the question or their response as a prompt for an unsent letter to the person they perceive as responsible for the relationship's breach. Then, continue the discussion in the sessions that follow.

 QUESTIONS FOR CLIENTS

Forgiveness can be a challenging issue in any relationship. Let's determine if forgiveness is the right step for you at this time:

- What does forgiveness mean to you?
- What are the pros and cons of forgiving the person who hurt you?
- How might you feel if you decide to forgive the person who hurt you?

MEDITATION SCRIPT FOR ANGER

Integrating guided meditations for anger into sessions can help provide clients with the support they may need to acknowledge and feel their anger. Just as importantly, however, guided meditations for anger can teach clients to extend themselves compassion, even in their anger.

Guided meditation for anger can also help to introduce your clients to the particular benefits of interrupting cycles of anger with the awareness enabled by meditation. As I point out above, anger can be a strong and seductive emotion. It may be easy for to feel anger, even if that ease isn't always recognized. Clients may consequently seek comfort in anger so as to avoid some of the more aching emotions and feelings associated with their loss, such as anguish and vulnerability.

Introduce the following meditation script to clients in session. Consider recording the session and offering clients the recording for their use at home or whenever they want to benefit from focusing in on their anger and allowing its expressions to move through them.

 ## MEDITATION SCRIPT FOR ANGER

Close your eyes and begin to take slow, even breaths. Let any sounds fall away. Let any random thoughts just drift off. Simply focus on your breath and the sound of my voice.

[Pause]

It's time to take a break, to relax, and to let yourself feel supported.

[Pause]

Acknowledge that you feel angry right now. Accept the way you feel. Remember that you have the power to control your reactions. You can experience anger, yet you can wait before you take action. You can be angry and also calm and in control.

[Pause]

Remind yourself that you are human and that you did not ask to be going through this experience. It's understandable that you have felt angry. You may also feel sad or scared too. That's okay.

[Pause]

Acknowledge your anger but also know that you are allowed to release it. You do not need to hold onto it if you no longer want to. With each exhale, imagine you are releasing your anger. You can feel it leaving your body and your heart.

[Pause]

Cultivate a feeling of compassion for yourself. See yourself as you would a friend or a child. Extend that same love to yourself. Forgive yourself. Trust yourself. Love yourself. Accept that you are having a difficult time and let that be okay.

[Pause]

Slowly begin to deepen your breath and come back into your body. Take your time opening your eyes and returning to the room.

MY ANGER PLAN

Developing an anger plan helps clients to identify the tools they can choose to use in response to their anger. As with the other plans offered in this workbook, no method will completely remove your clients' anger. However, a client's ability to formulate a plan is itself a testament to the work they have done to identify their expressions of anger, to feel their expressions of anger, and to cope with or manage their expressions of anger.

 CLIENT PLAN FOR ANGER

Let's reflect on the all the strategies for anger you have experimented with over the course of our work together. Draw on this work to help you answer the following prompts as fully and specifically as possible:

- When I feel angry, I will use these techniques to soothe myself . . .
- When I feel angry, I will call these people . . .
- When I feel angry, I will use this mindfulness technique . . .
- When I feel angry, I will use this meditation . . .

REFLECTION

I've found that anger can be a powerful and even seductive emotion in the grieving process. It is also one that grieving clients will likely experience at different times and for different reasons as they process their loss. This is why grieving clients benefit from sustained support in working with and through their anger. Although each client will experience anger in ways that are unique to them, the activities in this chapter will help all clients first acknowledge and identify their anger, then express and feel their anger, and ultimately, release it by letting it go.

CHAPTER 11

STRATEGIES FOR GUILT

Guilt is perhaps the most painful companion of death.

—**Elisabeth Kübler-Ross**

Guilt is a complex emotion, and it can manifest in many ways after the death of a loved one: Clients might feel guilt because they did not spend enough time with their loved one. They may feel they didn't value their loved one enough in life. They may think they could've or should've made different choices about a loved one's medical care. Or they might feel guilt for not recognizing, or perhaps not wanting to recognize, how close their loved one was to death.

Guilt can also arise as a consequence of unresolved issues or past hurts or arguments. Clients may feel that important things were left unsaid. They may also feel guilt that they suspect is not fully rational or deserved. This includes survivor's guilt and other types of guilt that may encourage clients to feel they were responsible in some way for their loved one's death.

In fact, it's rare to meet a client who doesn't feel a sense of guilt about something related to the death of their loved one. Guilt can be a reflexive response to the pain of loss. As with so many other emotions in the grieving process, guilt is often associated with the loss of control. Often, grieving people feel guilt because of their perceived responsibility over the circumstances of their loved one's death. Although many overestimate their influence on these circumstances, it is possible that something truly could have been done or said differently.

Because of its ubiquity, therapists and mental health professionals are familiar with the guilt attendant to loss. Some of us are more intimately familiar with these feelings of guilt. I know I am. After my mom died, I felt intense remorse. Because both my mother and father had a hard time talking about my mother's illness, I didn't understand how sick she truly was. And when my dad called to tell me that it was time to say goodbye, I started the long drive from my college to the hospital. At the last minute, I made a decision to stay with a friend for the night, and while I was there, my mom died. It's hard to describe the painful guilt and regret I experienced. I couldn't accept that I hadn't been there for her death and that I hadn't driven straight through the night to spend every possible moment with her. I worried that she didn't know how much I loved her, and I felt that I had not been a good enough daughter. For years, I was consumed with guilt about my lack of connection to her in those final weeks.

I found that in my case, and in the case of my clients, the guilt takes time to release. It's not something that necessarily disappears on its own. This may be because guilt allows clients, in its own strange way, to hold onto the person they've lost. Clients may feel—even if they don't *know* that they feel this way—that if they release our guilt, they are abandoning their grief or even their devotion to their person.

In this chapter, I introduce a variety of activities to help your clients feel and process their guilt. This includes activities to identify and work through guilt, and those to help clients find ways to understand, forgive, and accept the circumstances that contribute to their guilt and regret. As in the case of other emotions that can be difficult to express, such as anger, it is useful to introduce the activities for processing guilt in session, perhaps using prompts to open exploratory discussions. It is not always easy for clients to discuss guilt, even in a therapeutic environment. Once your clients have become comfortable identifying their own expressions of guilt, the activities can be completed as homework or used out of session to help clients reflect and process feelings of guilt on their own.

ACTIVITIES TO HELP CLIENTS IDENTIFY AND UNDERSTAND THEIR GUILT

Guilt may be a common response to the loss of a loved one, but when guilt is irrational, out of proportion to reality, directed inward, or a source of rumination, it can block clients' grieving process in unhealthy ways. As with anger, it isn't possible to simply make guilty feelings go away, but guilt can be expressed and released.

Constructively expressing and releasing guilt requires identification and the understanding of its provocations and sources. This is not easy in general, even in the most straightforward of circumstances. But when guilt is associated with death, it can be much more difficult.

The guilt your clients may feel after the death of their person can be multifaceted and can point in many directions. For many reasons, including those associated with shame, it can also be hard to acknowledge. Consequently, therapists and mental health professionals often need to support clients in identifying their guilt, which may mean helping them tease guilt apart from related expressions of grief, such as anxiety.

An exploratory discussion can act as an aid to identification. It can also provide an opportunity for education, destigmatization, and ultimately, normalization. Opening such a discussion can be fraught, however, because clients may find their guilt to be a particularly difficult topic of conversation. Perhaps they feel shame about their guilt, or perhaps they've had difficult conversations about guilt outside the therapeutic setting. It is not unusual for family members and friends to feel uncomfortable with a grieving person's guilt. This may be because guilt is a challenging emotion with no clear remedy.

Work with your clients to help them better understand and identify guilt's place in the grieving process. This can create a safer and more comfortable therapeutic atmosphere, allowing clients to reflect more deeply on, and potentially share, their emotions and feelings.

IDENTIFYING GUILT

Introduce your clients to the following psychological, physical, and spiritual symptoms of guilt. Symptoms of guilt overlap with many other symptoms, including symptoms of anxiety. This is one reason why it's important to help clients understand guilt and to support them as they reflect on the role of guilt in their own grieving process. It may be useful to pose hypothetical questions or questions based in curiosity, such as *What would it mean and how would it feel to consider guilt as a source of some of your symptoms?*

Psychological Symptoms of Guilt

- Experiencing recurring obsessive thoughts
- Feeling sad
- Feeling anxious
- Feeling anhedonia (an inability to feel pleasure or joy)
- Being sensitive to the effects of another's every action
- Feeling undeserving
- Neglecting your needs
- Depriving yourself
- Feeling overwhelmed by possibly making the "wrong" decision
- Experiencing low self-esteem
- Putting others before yourself to a detriment
- Avoiding your full range of emotions
- Ruminating on mistakes

Physical Symptoms of Guilt

- Insomnia or other sleep disturbances
- Indigestion or other stomach problems
- Fatigue and lethargy
- Muscle tension
- Sensation of heaviness in the body

Spiritual Symptoms of Guilt

- Inability to connect with higher power

- Inability to connect with sense of purpose

- Feeling lost and forsaken

- Projecting guilt onto higher power (e.g., "god is mad at me")

GUILT INVENTORY

Once clients gain familiarity with the symptoms associated with guilt, they may feel more prepared to discuss the prompts that make up the *Guilt Inventory*. While it may go without saying, it is important for me to remind clinicians to treat discussions about the *Guilt Inventory* with a great deal of sensitivity. The prompts can provoke a wide range of client responses. Some clients are able to speak frankly about their feelings of guilt. Others are not. While some clients may be able to easily categorize statements as irrelevant or inapplicable to their experiences, other clients may find it difficult, painful, or deeply upsetting to consider any of these prompts. For these clients, it can be useful to take breaks for deep breathing exercises or guided meditation, or you may want to encourage them to self-regulate by pausing to reconnect with their bodies and doing a few stretches or taking a sip of water.

Once clients understand and are able to consider each prompt, offer this inventory as a take-home assignment in preparation for tracking guilt and regret. As with the other inventories, repeating the *Guilt Inventory* in later sessions can be useful for helping clients identify patterns in their guilt, including potential triggers and effective coping mechanisms for specific symptoms. Repetition can also help clients name the ways in which they are learning to manage their anger, and to seek support as they continue to process their loss.

GUILT INVENTORY

Put a check mark by the following sentences that apply to your own experience of guilt.

- ☐ I was responsible for what happened.
- ☐ I caused what happened.
- ☐ I blame myself for what happened.
- ☐ I could have prevented what happened.
- ☐ I should have made different choices.
- ☐ I blame myself for something I thought, did, or felt.
- ☐ I knew the right thing to do but didn't do it.
- ☐ I had thoughts or beliefs I shouldn't have had.
- ☐ I had feelings I shouldn't have had.
- ☐ I did something that went against my values.
- ☐ I was selfish.
- ☐ I need to feel guilty.
- ☐ I will never forgive myself.
- ☐ I will someday forgive myself.
- ☐ I did something wrong, and I am a bad person.
- ☐ I did something wrong, but I am still a good person.

GUILT AND REGRET TRACKING JOURNAL

Although acknowledging guilt and regret can bring up painful feelings for everyone, the stakes of acknowledging guilt and regret for grieving people may feel close to life and death. Some clients may be unable to acknowledge or express their guilt and regret, resulting in blockage that cannot help but manifest in a variety of the symptoms described in the previous section.

The tracking journal encourages clients to become aware of the ways in which their guilt and regret manifests in their day-to-day lives. By helping to externalize their guilt and regret, the worksheet also opens up ways for clients to accept and process it. After discussing the *Guilt Inventory*, send this worksheet template home with clients and then review it in session each week.

GUILT AND REGRET TRACKING JOURNAL

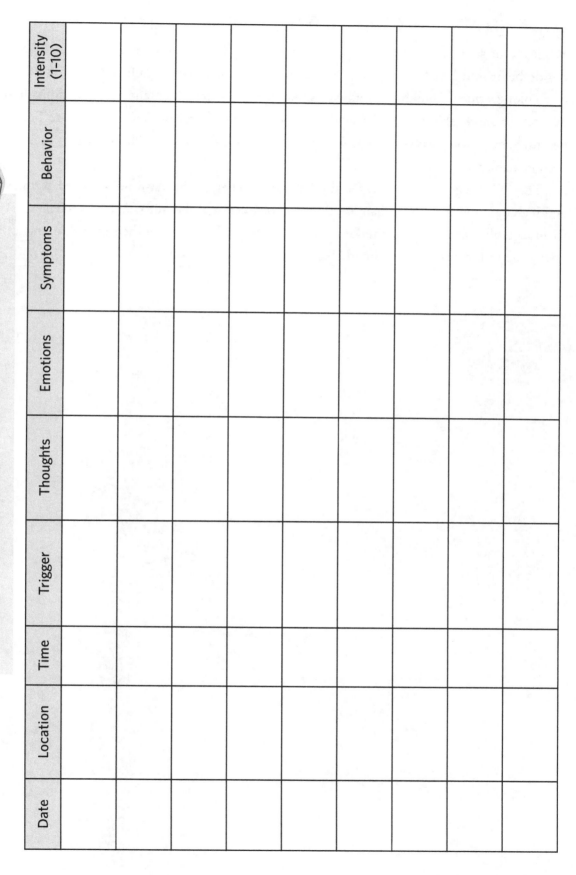

Date	Location	Time	Trigger	Thoughts	Emotions	Symptoms	Behavior	Intensity (1-10)

GUILT-RELATED THINKING ERRORS

While clients sometimes experience guilt and regret as a rational response to things that they did or did not do before our loved one's death, they often experience irrational guilt and regret as a consequence of thinking errors. Thinking errors can strengthen misperceptions and make it difficult to gain a broader or more objective understanding of the grieving process. These errors are pervasive, and because they provide access to an easy-to-grasp reason for feelings of guilt and regret, they can quickly become habitual.

The following handout is especially helpful for clients who have unexamined feelings of guilt and regret around the loss of their loved one. Explain each of the thinking errors to clients. Then, ask them to explore which of the thinking errors may be guiding some of their own thinking, potentially giving rise to (or sustaining) guilt and regret.

GUILT-RELATED THINKING ERRORS

Review the following thinking errors as a way to consider reframing your thoughts and beliefs.

- **Are you experiencing hindsight bias?** This occurs when our impression of how we acted or would have acted changes after we learn the outcome of an event. In the case of a loved one's death, this bias can lead us to believe that we knew what was going to happen or that we overlooked signals that we should have been able to interpret. Our biased beliefs can even lead us to believe that we caused or could have prevented our person's death. Ask yourself: What did I know then? What do I know now? How can I differentiate between the two?

- **Are you exaggerating your role?** We inadvertently exaggerate our role when we spotlight our individual contribution to significant events. This leads us to assume we had an outsized impact on the outcome. It also leads us to overlook the roles played by other people. When we exaggerate our role, we often assume that we, more than anyone else, are responsible for the circumstances of our loved one's death. Ask yourself: How would an objective eyewitness describe my role?

- **Are you confusing prevention with causation?** Sometimes when we feel that we could have prevented an outcome, we believe that we also caused the outcome. However, prevention and causation are very different things. This thinking error is often complicated by our tendency to *both* exaggerate our role *and* to confuse prevention with causation. In this case, we distort our understanding of our own ability to prevent events, and we also assume our distorted role is evidence of causation. Ask yourself: Can I explain the difference between "preventing" something and "causing" it?

- **Are you experiencing accountability guilt?** Those of us who hold accountable roles, like parents or caregivers, sometimes believe that we are completely responsible for our loved ones' safety in all circumstances, whether or not we have control over—or are even fully aware of—those circumstances. When a loved one dies, we believe we had the power to prevent this outcome. When we develop this belief, we ignore what was actually foreseeable and possible. Ask yourself: Can anyone keep anyone else safe in all circumstances? Can I expect my own parent or caregiver to keep me safe at all times?

- **Are you ignoring the reality of pressured decision-making?** No matter our role, when we're under pressure or in the midst of an emergency, our actions are informed by freeze, fight, or flight responses. In these circumstances, we may make different decisions than we'd otherwise make. These are normal and expected reactions to stressful situations. Ask yourself: What pressures did I feel during the circumstances of my loved one's death?

- **Were you aware of other options that were available to you?** We often feel guilt after the death of a loved one for decisions we did *not* make, even when we did not know all of our options at the time. This thinking error overlooks the reality of constrained choices. Whether we recognize it or not, our choices are always limited by external variables. Further, we can't always be aware of all of our options all of the time. In hindsight, we often forget that our knowledge was more limited at the time than it is now. Ask yourself: Did I make the best decision given the knowledge I had at the time?

- **Are you holding yourself to unreasonable standards?** Sometimes we hold ourselves to impossible standards or entertain fantasies that we could have acted in a way that was not truly possible. This thinking error informs many of the preceding thinking errors, as well. Ask yourself: Are my standards for my actions reasonable? Can I identify anyone else who I think should also be able to meet these standards?

- **Are you engaging in counterfactual thinking?** This kind of thinking occurs when we focus on possible alternatives to life events that have already happened. These thoughts consist of "what ifs" and "if onlys." Counterfactual thinking can lead to rumination, and we may fixate on alternative realities that were not possible at the time and are not possible now. Ask yourself: What are my "what ifs" and "if onlys"?

- **Are you feeling hunch regret?** Hunch regret is a dimension of hindsight bias in which we believe, after an event has occurred, that we should have seen it coming or that we overlooked signs that indicated the event. In some ways, hunch regret relates to the confusion between prevention and causation. It's important to acknowledge that even if we had a hunch or gut feeling about what would happen, that doesn't mean we could have or even should have acted on it. Identifying and acting on a hunch does not mean that an outcome would have been prevented. Ask yourself: Do I feel like I had a hunch that something bad was going to happen? In what ways were my decisions and actions constrained?

- **Are you ignoring your intentions?** When we place the blame on ourselves for an undesirable outcome, we often overlook our intentions. Ask yourself: Did I intend for a bad outcome?

- **Are you confusing a feeling with evidence?** Confusing a feeling with evidence is a common experience. In the case of a loved one's death, it can be a source of a great deal of pain. Just because you feel guilty does not mean that you are. Your guilt may be related to a number of other things. In fact, it might be a way for you to hold on to your loved one. Ask yourself: What evidence do I have that supports my guilt?

ACTIVITIES FOR MANAGING AND COPING WITH GUILT

Thinking errors provide salient, seemingly rationale explanations for feelings of guilt. However, thinking errors are based on misperceptions. As clients become familiar with thinking errors and how their own misperceptions inform these errors, they become more capable of introducing interventions.

CHANGING SELF-PERCEPTIONS

The *Changing Self-Perceptions* worksheet helps to encourage new, more constructive thinking habits. This activity does not ask clients to stop feeling guilt; it simply asks them to dissociate their feelings of guilt from a rationale.

Consider introducing this worksheet to clients during a session, using the common thinking errors you have already discussed to establish examples of misperceptions and reframed perceptions. Then, ask clients to reframe the misperceptions they frequently experience. Encourage them to fill out the worksheet several times a day, and then ask them to share their experiences during their next session.

CHANGING SELF-PERCEPTIONS

Use your knowledge of thinking errors to identify the misperceptions in your self-talk. Then, work to reframe each of these misperceptions. Integrate this worksheet into your daily life by adding to it once or twice a day. Then, continue to add to it as often as required to reframe misperceptions.

Misperceptions	Reframed Perceptions
I should have known better.	I did the best I could at the time.

FLIP THE SCRIPT ON GUILT

Misperceptions and thinking errors can powerfully inform the grieving process and can be difficult for clients to release. For those clients who feel lost in grief, pain and other feelings associated with guilt can feel like an appropriate consequence of the loss of their loved one. However, guilt can also provide a kind of comfort. Rather than accepting the difficult reality that many circumstances are outside their control and that some things happen that don't make sense, guilt allows clients to assign blame. This may sound strange, but assigning blame for pain can actually help to make sense of some of the most difficult, confusing experiences.

For these reasons, it can be difficult to support clients in processing and then letting go of their guilt. The *Flip the Script on Guilt* worksheet offers a critical tool, guiding clients to tell themselves a different story. Ask them to complete the worksheet outside of session, and then discuss their experience completing it, exploring any of the difficulties they might have experienced.

FLIP THE SCRIPT ON GUILT

Answer the following questions with as much detail as possible.

Write down all the negative and critical things you think about yourself in regard to your guilt. Go into detail about how ashamed and flawed you feel.

_____

_____

_____

_____

_____

_____

_____

_____

Now think of the nicest, most compassionate person you know. Write down what they would say to you in response to your previous answer.

_____

_____

_____

_____

_____

_____

_____

_____

_____

SURVIVOR'S GUILT

Survivor's guilt is a common feeling after a loss. It often manifests when clients have survived a traumatic event in which other people died. It may occur if clients feel they didn't do enough to save others who died, or if their own life was saved (or they feel their own life was saved) by another person who died. Some people may experience survivor's guilt simply because they remain alive after their loved one's death, even when they are not a survivor of the particular circumstances in which their loved one died.

While survivor's guilt can show up as anxiety, a number of related symptoms accompany survivor's guilt as well, including:

- Flashbacks

- Sleeplessness

- Helplessness

- Suicidality

- Fear and anxiety

- Irritability

- Depression

Survivor's guilt can be pervasive and requires identification and reframing. Accordingly, clients may benefit from an exploratory discussion about survivor's guilt.

QUESTIONS FOR CLIENTS

Let's explore your guilt concerning your loved one's death:

- Do you feel guilty about being the one who is alive?
- Do you feel guilty about something you failed to do that you believe could have changed the outcome?
- Do you feel guilty about a choice you made or action you took?

Clients who are able to identify their survivor's guilt and who are experiencing one or more of the associated symptoms will benefit from a discussion of the questions in this section. These questions should begin as an in-session conversation, so that clients can be supported as they consider the circumstances surrounding the death of their person and their role in those circumstances.

(?) QUESTIONS FOR CLIENTS

Let's consider your role in your loved one's death:

- What could you have done differently to truly change the outcome?
- Did you have time or enough emotional bandwidth to make a sound decision?
- Did you make the best decision you could, given the circumstances and the knowledge you had at the time?
- What responsibility do others have for the outcome?
- How does holding onto your guilt serve you?
- Would the person you lost forgive you for the choices you made?

It is important to first introduce this dialogue in session so that clients don't inadvertently reinforce the story they're accustomed to telling themselves about their loved one's death. This is typically a story in which their guilt as a survivor is warranted.

Most people, whether or not they are grieving, find it relatively easy to believe the stories they tell themselves in their heads. They often need to speak these stories aloud to be able to identify their inconsistencies. Consequently, by introducing this as an in-session activity, you can foster a dialogue that allows clients to articulate their beliefs aloud and to listen to your responses. As you listen, gently consider any misperceptions or errors that may be supporting their survivor's guilt.

Once you have helped your clients identify the more objective reality of their role as a survivor, you can ask them to reflect further on the questions and respond more fully to them outside of session. They can then bring back their answers for further discussion.

RELATIONSHIP GUILT RELEASE

Clients may also feel guilt associated with their relationship with their loved one. Sometimes a client may feel that their last moments with their loved one did not accurately attest to their love for their person. Maybe a client and their person were fighting, and the client said things they wish they hadn't. Maybe a client didn't have time for their loved one or didn't prioritize them or their needs. Maybe a client was estranged from their loved one at the time of death.

There are many reasons why clients might feel relationship guilt after their loved one's death. To help them move through this kind of guilt, offer them the following steps for release.

IN-SESSION ACTIVITY

Use the following steps when you feel guilty:

1. Let yourself grieve the relationship itself.
2. Review the reasons for the relationship strain.

3. If there were boundaries in place, remind yourself of why.

4. Journal or write letters to your person as a way of making amends, seeking forgiveness, or saying things you didn't get a chance to say.

5. Choose to forgive yourself or them for the strained relationship.

JOURNAL PROMPTS FOR GUILT AND REGRET

The prompts below help clients go deeper into their answers from the preceding activities to better understand their guilt and regret and locate its sources. Guilt and regret do not usually go away on their own, but as clients learn more about their guilt, including whether they feel it acts as a proxy for their bond with their loved one, they can more easily manage and process it.

 JOURNAL PROMPTS

Use the prompts that speak to you to begin to identify, acknowledge, and fully feel your guilt and regret more comprehensively:

- I feel ashamed about . . .
- I regret . . .
- Something I wish I had done differently is . . .
- If I could go back, I would . . .
- I am hard on myself because . . .
- My guilt is irrational because . . .
- If I could tell my loved one something, I would say . . .
- If I could talk to my younger self, I would say . . .
- My guilt is affecting my life by . . .
- My guilt can teach me about myself by . . .
- I can use my guilt to help me grow by . . .
- I can use my guilt as a motivation to help others by . . .
- Something that is holding me back from moving on is . . .
- Forgiving myself would feel like . . .
- I deserve forgiveness because . . .
- Something I need to heal is . . .

LETTER WRITING FOR GUILT

Fully acknowledging and expressing guilt is an important step in processing and releasing it. Journal writing and letter writing can offer an opportunity for your clients to fully express their guilt and remorse, even when that guilt and remorse seems irrational.

This may feel like sensitive territory: After all, you don't want to inadvertently reinforce the stories that your clients may tell themselves to perpetuate their sense of guilt. Yet, many clients feel so buried by their guilt, whether or not it seems appropriate or well-founded to outside observers, that they simply move forward in processing their grief without fully expressing their guilty feelings. For this reason, it's often useful and even necessary to encourage grieving clients to write to the person or entity to whom they feel the most guilt so as to fully express the emotions they feel inside.

As with letters for grief and anger, this letter is not for sending. Clients can write what they need to write, to anyone or anything, without worrying about hurting the recipient.

 ## LETTER WRITING

Writing letters about your guilt can be a healthy way to express it. These are not letters to be sent—they are just for you. Write them in a journal or on a computer. Tell the person or the entity why you are angry and describe your feelings.

Try writing letters to:

- The person who died
- Family members
- Friends
- Medical personnel
- Yourself
- Your younger self
- Your future self

MAKING AMENDS WITH YOURSELF

After clients have fully expressed their guilt, they can turn toward making amends. The act of making amends is designed to help them release their feelings of guilt, which will then free them to continue moving through their grieving process. Much like letter writing, this worksheet allows the grieving individual to ask for—and grant themselves—the forgiveness they believe they need.

MAKING AMENDS WITH YOURSELF

Write out what you want to say to your loved one or to the person about whom you feel guilt.

I'm sorry for _____

_____

_____

_____

_____

I was wrong because _____

_____

_____

_____

_____

Next time I will _____

_____

_____

_____

_____

I deserve forgiveness because _____

_____

_____

_____

_____

LETTING GO OF GUILT

Feelings of guilt and blame can be difficult incredibly difficult to release, in part because grieving individuals often experience guilt and blame as proxies for intimacy with their loved one who has died. To continue supporting your clients as they work to let go of feelings of guilt and blame, guide them through the *Letting Go of Guilt* worksheet in session. Then, ask them to continue to reflect on the questions and fill out the questions more completely on their own.

LETTING GO OF GUILT

Answer the questions below, including as much detail as possible, to help let go of the guilt and blame you feel.

What are you blaming yourself for?

_____

_____

_____

_____

_____

Is your guilt rational or irrational? Explain.

_____

_____

_____

_____

_____

How do you cope with your guilt?

_____

_____

_____

_____

_____

What would it feel like to forgive yourself?

_____

_____

_____

_____

_____

How can you begin to forgive yourself?

_____

_____

_____

_____

_____

Why do you deserve forgiveness?

_____

_____

_____

_____

_____

MEDITATION SCRIPT FOR GUILT AND REGRET

Integrating guided meditations for guilt into sessions can help provide clients with the support they may need to safely process their guilt, as well as to extend themselves compassion for their guilty feelings and to begin to tell new stories of forgiveness. Guided meditation for guilt can also help to introduce your clients to the particular benefits of interrupting cycles of guilt—especially ruminative guilt—with the awareness enabled by meditation.

As I point out above, guilt, like anger, can be a strong and seductive emotion. It may even be easy for clients to feel guilt, even if that ease isn't always recognized. Clients may consequently seek a kind of comfort in their guilty feelings because guilt (like anxiety and anger) can provide a relative refuge from the more upsetting emotions and feelings associated with their loss.

Introduce the following meditation script to clients in session. Consider recording the session and offering clients the recording for their use at home or whenever they want to benefit from focusing in on their guilt and allowing its expressions to move through them.

MEDITATION SCRIPT FOR GUILT AND REGRET

Close your eyes and begin to take slow, even breaths. Let any sounds fall away. Let any random thoughts just drift off. Simply focus on your breath and the sound of my voice.

[Pause]

To practice this meditation, we are going to call up your grief and all the pain and regret you are feeling. We are going to call to attention everything you are struggling with and all the remorse you are feeling. I want you to fully acknowledge that you are in a moment of suffering.

[Pause]

I want you to bring into focus something you regret. Just for now, just during this meditation, I want to ask you to release your regret. I want to ask you to forgive yourself.

[Pause]

I want to ask you to view yourself with compassion and kindness. I want you to forgive yourself for your mistakes. Remind yourself that you are human. That we all make mistakes. That we all deserve forgiveness and compassion.

[Pause]

I want you to imagine what it would feel like to release your guilt and regret. Imagine what your body and your world will feel like without this burden.

[Pause]

I want you to imagine that you are forgiven by anyone you feel that you have hurt. They forgive you. They release you. They see you with kindness and love and compassion.

[Pause]

You are worthy of releasing this regret. You are a good person. You are a human. You are full of love and kindness.

[Pause]

Say to yourself: May I be kind to myself. May I accept my flaws. May I forgive myself. May I be strong. May I feel compassion for myself.

[Pause]

Slowly begin to deepen your breath and come back into your body. Take your time opening your eyes and returning to the room.

REFLECTION

Guilt and remorse are like anxiety and anger. They can be powerful and even seductive emotions and feelings in the grieving process. They can help a grieving person make sense of what has happened and explain why they feel so bad. However, guilt can also immobilize the grieving process, preventing clients from experiencing other necessary emotions as they move through the experience of loss. Grieving clients often require strong and sustained support to work through their guilt. Although each client will experience guilt in ways that are unique to them, the activities in this chapter will help all clients acknowledge and identify their guilt, ultimately allowing them to express and feel it in order to let it go.

CHAPTER 12

CULTIVATING SELF-COMPASSION AND RESILIENCE

Talk to yourself like you would talk to someone you love.

—**Brené Brown**

Although self-compassion is a healing gift we can give ourselves, many of us find it difficult to extend this kind of compassion. When we experience feelings or emotions that cause us discomfort, we often find it easier to reproach or berate ourselves rather than express kindness and care.

Self-compassion is important for everybody, but it's critical for grieving individuals. As your clients encounter and process their grief and associated anxiety, anger, and guilt, they begin to adjust to their lives without their person. This transition can be freeing: It signals a shift from simply surviving the pain of early grief to the more empowering work of learning to live with the loss. However, the shift is also fraught. Clients feel relief when emerging from their most intense experiences of grief, but they often perceive the intensity of their grief as a reflection of their intimacy with their loved one. They may feel that their movement through the grieving process means they will be leaving their loved one behind.

To support your clients, help them embrace the new version of themselves that is emerging. This requires helping them express self-compassion as they move through their grieving process and begin to build new supports in their lives. While self-compassion sustains clients as they grieve, it also fosters resilience, or the ability to weather the storms of grief no matter how much they dare to buffet. Resiliency means that your clients are able to take care of themselves, but they can only do this when they're able to express deep compassion for their experiences.

In this chapter, I introduce a variety of activities for helping clients to foster self-compassion and resilience. The activities are mutually reinforcing: Self-kindness enables recovery by fostering inner strength. The activities that follow can be used during sessions to support clients as they learn strategies for cultivating self-compassion and resilience. Clients may also benefit from completing the activities on their own so as to deepen their engagement through sustained reflection. However you choose to use the activities, they will help clients move with empathy and courage through their grieving process.

ACTIVITIES TO HELP CLIENTS CULTIVATE SELF-COMPASSION

Cultivating self-compassion is a skill, and as such, it can be learned. In fact, because self-compassion is such a crucial support in the grieving process, it's important to mount an ongoing effort to help clients integrate the activities in this section into their daily lives.

Clients sometimes find it difficult to illustrate their expressions of self-compassion with relevant examples. This is a common issue for grieving, anxiously grieving, and non-grieving clients alike. Many people feel perfectly confident in their ability to express compassion to someone else—to lend a hand or an ear to a friend in need—but they may find it far more challenging to do this for themselves. To begin to help clients create a lifelong habit of cultivating self-compassion, it is useful to define the basics of self-compassion and open a discussion about its variations.

IDENTIFYING SELF-COMPASSION

Self-compassion refers to the awareness of our own distress and a corollary desire and ability to alleviate it. Conceptually, however, self-compassion is the sum of three parts: mindfulness, connectedness, and self-kindness. Each of these parts is necessary for the expression of self-compassion. It may be useful, therefore, to discuss with clients examples of each part that you've observed over the course of your work together.

- **Mindfulness:** Being present to your thoughts, feelings, and circumstances

- **Connectedness:** Allowing yourself to feel connected to humanity and remembering that everyone experiences suffering

- **Self-kindness:** Expressing love and compassion toward yourself

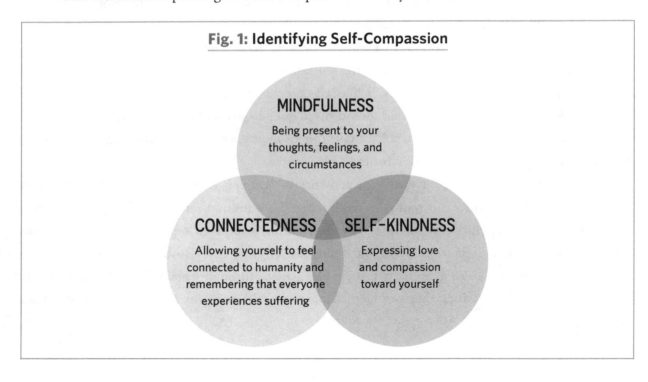

Fig. 1: Identifying Self-Compassion

MINDFULNESS
Being present to your thoughts, feelings, and circumstances

CONNECTEDNESS
Allowing yourself to feel connected to humanity and remembering that everyone experiences suffering

SELF-KINDNESS
Expressing love and compassion toward yourself

SELF-COMPASSION INVENTORY

As clients gain a more nuanced understanding of self-compassion, they can identify the strength of their self-compassion skills. The *Self-Compassion Inventory* offers a tool for this work, giving you and your clients a broad view of their current practice of self-compassion and helping to point toward the activities that will best support ongoing efforts at its cultivation.

SELF-COMPASSION INVENTORY

Put a check mark by the following statements that describe your experience with self-compassion.

- ☐ I am generally satisfied with myself.
- ☐ I am constantly hard on myself.
- ☐ I feel angry at myself when I make mistakes or fail.
- ☐ I have qualities that I am proud of.
- ☐ I fixate on things I do wrong.
- ☐ When I do something wrong, I remind myself that no one is perfect.
- ☐ I feel that I am a worthwhile person.
- ☐ I often feel inadequate.
- ☐ I try to be kind to myself when I am in pain.
- ☐ When I'm feeling down, I think other people must be happier than me.
- ☐ I feel good about who I am.
- ☐ When I am upset, I make efforts to manage my emotions in healthy ways.
- ☐ When I notice things I don't like about myself, I feel angry and depressed.
- ☐ I feel alone in my failures.
- ☐ I am tolerant of my flaws.
- ☐ Most people are better at life than I am.
- ☐ I will never be enough.
- ☐ I am often disappointed with myself.
- ☐ I feel love for myself.
- ☐ I accept myself as I am.

HOW WOULD YOU TREAT A FRIEND?

To begin to identify specific expressions of self-compassion, grieving clients can complete the *How Would You Treat a Friend?* worksheet. In my discussions with clients about self-compassion, I'm always surprised—and sometimes even startled—by the difference between the ways that clients describe treating their friends and the ways clients describe treating themselves.

Perhaps I really shouldn't be surprised. When I reflect back on my own grieving process, especially after my mom's death, I remember urging myself to get over my feelings of sadness and to move on with my life. I seldom allowed myself to sit with my difficult feelings. When I did, I certainly didn't respond to those feelings with kindness. More often than not, I responded with impatience. I would never have treated a friend the way I treated myself.

This worksheet helps to draw a client's attention to this potential disparity. It also asks them to consider how they act toward friends to better identify what expressions of self-compassion the client themselves may want and need. Introduce this worksheet in session, supporting clients as they approach what might feel like difficult work. Then, encourage clients to reflect on the questions at home and to bring back their responses for further discussion.

HOW WOULD YOU TREAT A FRIEND?

Answer the following questions with as much detail as possible.

Think about times when a close friend is struggling with something or feels bad about themselves. How would you respond to them? Describe the things you typically say, the actions you take, and the compassion you feel for them.

_____

_____

_____

_____

_____

_____

_____

Think about times when you are struggling with something or feeling bad about yourself. Describe what you typically do, think, and feel in these moments.

_____

_____

_____

_____

_____

_____

_____

Describe the differences between how you react to your friends as opposed to yourself. What do you think leads you to treat yourself and others differently?

_____

_____

_____

_____

_____

_____

Describe how you could respond to yourself more like you respond to your friend. What could you say and do differently? How you could show yourself compassion?

_____

_____

_____

_____

_____

_____

Describe what would change if you responded to yourself the way you respond to your friends.

_____

_____

_____

_____

_____

_____

_____

REFRAMING NEGATIVE SELF-TALK

Sometimes, rather than offering ourselves self-compassion, we criticize ourselves instead. This is a common habit, and it certainly isn't limited to grieving clients. Many people habitually deride their emotions, feelings, and behaviors rather than viewing them through a more neutral lens. In doing this, they withhold kindness from themselves, often when they need it the most.

Learning how to reframe critical self-talk is an essential part of cultivating self-compassion and is an especially helpful skill for grieving clients and those with grief anxiety. When clients who are processing a loss criticize themselves, they are denying themselves the compassion they need. When they repeatedly criticize themselves for their experiences of grief, their expressions of grief can become blocked.

Introduce the *Reframing Negative Self-Talk* activity in session to help clients identify their criticisms and the rationale informing those criticisms. They may not even be aware of these criticisms, as they have become so habitual in their day-to-day life. This discussion can be both educational and empowering: Sometimes, simply spelling out their internalized critique surprises clients, enabling them to intervene. Once the client has practiced this reframing, they can continue using this activity outside of session.

IN-SESSION ACTIVITY

Each time you find yourself being hard on yourself, use these questions to help yourself reframe your negative self-talk:

- What am I being hard on myself about?
- What are the critical things I am saying to myself?
- How do I feel when I say those things to myself?
- What are some forgiving and compassionate things I could say to myself instead?

MINDFULNESS FOR SELF-COMPASSION

As the preceding activities help to make clear, many behaviors that support self-criticism are internal or habitual. The ability of mindfulness to gently focus your clients' attention on their internal experiences helps in the cultivation of self-compassion.

The *Mindfulness for Self-Compassion* activity can be something you and your clients routinely complete every session, or you can complete it with them when you notice that they are feeling activated or are expressing criticism about an aspect of their grief or grieving process. With repeated practice, many clients will create new habits and behaviors around patterns of critique, such that their critique acts as a cue for mindfulness.

IN-SESSION ACTIVITY

Use the following steps to cultivate a mindful moment of self-compassion:

1. Recognize that the present moment is painful and that you are suffering. Try not to dismiss your feelings; instead, recognize them as part of your truth.

2. Remind yourself that suffering and pain are unavoidable parts of life. Everyone experiences moments like this. You are not alone in what you are going through.

3. Repeat a mantra to yourself such as:
   - *It's okay that I'm having a hard time.*
   - *May I be kind to myself.*
   - *May I receive the support I need.*
   - *I accept myself as I am.*
   - *I have compassion for myself.*

LETTER WRITING FOR SELF-COMPASSION

I introduced letter writing as a means for processing emotions and feelings pertaining to grief, anger, and guilt. Not surprisingly, this is also a beneficial activity for expressing self-compassion as well. As I've described, writing (but not sending) letters to others can provide an outlet for articulating emotions and feelings that are otherwise hard to express. Writing letters to *ourselves* can be a powerful way to practice talking to ourselves in understanding and forgiving ways.

Introduce the *Letter Writing for Self-Compassion* activity in session once clients have identified their behaviors around expressing self-compassion and have practiced extending themselves kindness and forgiveness.

 **LETTER WRITING**

When you are feeling bad about yourself or being hard on yourself, try writing a letter following these steps:

1. Begin by bringing to mind whatever it is you are being hard on yourself about. You might write about how you think you should be stronger, you should grieve more, or you should feel less angry.

2. Now write a letter to yourself from the perspective of a friend or someone who deeply cares for and loves you. Try to imagine what they would say to you, how they might comfort you, and all the ways they would be understanding of your feelings.

AFFIRMATIONS FOR SELF-COMPASSION

When it comes to expressing self-compassion, many clients find that the affirmations for grief, discussed in chapter 8 are useful. Clients may also find that a simple validating statement, such as I accept myself as I am, can be an effective reminder to show themselves the same kindness they would show a struggling friend.

 AFFIRMATIONS FOR CLIENTS

Repeat these affirmations whenever you need some self-compassion:

- It's okay to make mistakes.
- I'm doing the best I can.
- I don't need to change myself to love myself.

- _____

MEDITATION SCRIPT FOR SELF-COMPASSION

This meditation script echoes some of the elements of the previous scripts for grief and anger. All of the scripts in this book are mutually reinforcing, acclimating grieving clients to meditation and deepening their engagement with meditation practices.

Introduce the following meditation script in session to clients. Consider recording the session and offering clients the recording for their use at home or whenever they want to benefit from focusing in on their self-compassion and allowing expressions of kindness to move through them.

 MEDITATION SCRIPT FOR SELF-COMPASSION

Close your eyes and begin to take slow, even breaths. Let any sounds fall away. Let any random thoughts just drift off. Simply focus on your breath and the sound of my voice.

[Pause]

To practice this meditation, we are going to call up your grief and all the pain you are feeling. We are going to call to attention everything you are struggling with. I want you to fully acknowledge that you are in a moment of suffering.

[Pause]

I want you to feel kindness and compassion toward yourself. Even if it's just for this one moment, allow yourself to feel kindness and compassion that you are going through this very human experience. View yourself as you would a child or a dear friend. What kind of love and kindness would you extend to them? Cultivate that same love and compassion for yourself. Let it wash over and through you. Let it comfort you.

[Pause]

Remind yourself that you are human. That it's okay to feel all that you are feeling. That you did not ask for this experience and that you are doing your very best to get through it. Again, take time to feel tenderness toward yourself.

[Pause]

Remind yourself that you are supported as you move through your grief. You are safe and you are loved and you are not alone. You are a human doing the very best that you can.

[Pause]

Say to yourself: May I be kind to myself. May I begin to accept myself as I am. May I forgive myself. May I be strong. May I be patient. May I receive support. Finally, may I find compassion for this me in this moment in time.

[Pause]

Slowly begin to deepen your breath and come back into your body. Take your time opening your eyes and returning to the room.

ACTIVITIES TO HELP CLIENTS CULTIVATE RESILIENCE

Although resilience is not always an explicit part of the conversation around cultivating self-compassion, it is one important consequence of treating ourselves with kindness and care. When clients offer themselves patience and love, they learn that they can give themselves what they need, even when that might be difficult.

Connecting resilience to self-compassion is particularly useful because the concept of resilience, as it relates to grief, can otherwise be tricky. There are many points along the journey of loss when a grieving person wants nothing to do with rebuilding and embracing life after their loved one is gone. In fact, the idea can seem offensive or can make them feel as though they are forcing themselves to move on from their loss and grief.

When clients have lost someone close to them, they might feel it is impossible to imagine ever wanting to be happy again. The idea of thriving or of ever being okay without their person can conjure up feelings of betrayal. For some, the goals associated with resilience might equate to a feeling of letting go.

Even so, there comes a point in the grief journey at which clients can make choices about how they will move forward in their lives now that their loved one is no longer here. In her best-selling memoir *The Angel in My Pocket*, author Sukey Forbes writes about the loss of her six-year-old daughter:

> What was I going to do? The choices seemed basic and slim: Die. Exist. Live. I wanted
> to die, but with two young children to care for and a husband, that wasn't an option.

Exist. I could do that. I was doing that now. But how flat and lifeless. How dreary and endless the long march would be until I met Charlotte again. The only option that resonated with me was to live. But how? I wanted to want to live. That was the best I could do in that moment.

This is how I've come to think of resilience—it's the choice we make to live.

It is important to acknowledge that many people go through a loss so great that they only ever feel capable of existence. They simply cannot choose to live. This is the best they can do. For others, however, resilience offers a way to not just survive their loss but to learn how to live again alongside it.

As a therapist or mental health professional, your role in cultivating your clients' resilience is often in helping them to understand that choosing resilience does not mean they are choosing to "let go" of their loved one or to "move on" from their grief. Resilience is about finding a balance. It's about your clients allowing themselves to grieve *and* to live. To do this, they must have a base level of self-compassion.

All humans are capable of resilience. It's important to note, though, that a person who demonstrates little emotional stress when faced with difficulty is not necessarily resilient. It's the person who is suffering, and who sometimes fails but continues to try, who displays resilience. Some people may be more resilient than others, but like self-compassion, resilience is not a fixed trait. Instead, it is a learned ability and one that can be built.

RESILIENCE INVENTORY

The *Resilience Inventory* offers broad insight into your client's experience of resilience. To conduct the inventory, give your clients the following worksheet. If they have difficulty identifying or recognizing their resilience, use the questions as the basis for a more dynamic in-session discussion.

Repeating the inventory in later sessions can also be useful in helping clients to identify the ways in which their resilience has changed and grown.

RESILIENCE INVENTORY

Put a check mark by the following statements that describe your current experience.

- ☐ I usually manage to get through difficult times.
- ☐ I am able to depend on myself.
- ☐ I am able to accept help from others.
- ☐ I am self-sufficient.
- ☐ Making friends comes easily to me.
- ☐ It does not take me long to recover from a stressful event.
- ☐ Staying interested in things is important to me.
- ☐ I am proud of my accomplishments.
- ☐ Past successes give me confidence.
- ☐ I feel like I can handle a lot.
- ☐ I have self-discipline.
- ☐ When I make plans, I follow through with them.
- ☐ I look for creative ways to solve problems.
- ☐ I believe in myself.
- ☐ I am open to new experiences.
- ☐ I can handle unpleasant feelings.
- ☐ I am not easily discouraged by failure.
- ☐ I accept change easily.
- ☐ My life has meaning.
- ☐ I am determined to overcome obstacles.

FOUR THEMES OF RESILIENCE

Resilient grieving refers to finding strength in the face of loss. When clients choose the path of resilient grieving, they choose to keep working toward gaining the coping tools that will help them find meaning even in their loss. For clients who want to choose resilient grieving, you can foster resilient grieving in four categories.

Resilient Thinking

Resilient thinking helps grieving clients shift from negative, ruminative thinking patterns to thought patterns that better support and soothe their grief. Resilient thinking is emphatically not positive thinking: It does not require that clients look at the so-called bright side of their grief or to consider what they may have gained in their loss. Instead, resilient thinking encourages clients to refocus their attention from an isolating fixation on the pain of loss and instead courageously accept their loss, experience the painful feelings of their loss, and foster the thoughts that will support and soothe them in their grief.

Supportive Relationships

Supportive relationships are important for everybody because they foster the ability to ask for and receive help. However, supportive relationships are critical to grieving clients. It's quite common for grieving individuals to avoid asking for the help they need. They may feel their requests are too big or too complicated. They may struggle to identify or articulate what they need. Working with clients to identify, foster, and rely on their supportive relationships reinforces their resilient grieving, in part by helping to communicate that clients can often find and receive help from others.

Emotion Management

Emotion management in resilient grieving refers to the commitment to work with the emotions that arise as a consequence of a loss. As with resilient thinking, emotion management in no way suggests grieving and anxiously grieving clients must turn their attention from their painful, volatile, upsetting emotions or the emotions that make them feel vulnerable. On the contrary, emotion management refers to attending to each emotion, allowing its expression, and responding to it with care and measures of comfort. Clients are most capable of emotion management when they take care of their physical and mental well-being. This means attending to healthy eating and regular exercise and practicing mindfulness and meditation. Working with clients on emotion management requires encouraging the self-care of their body and mind so they are capable of encountering the emotions that arise as they grieve.

Building on Strengths

Building on strengths refers to encouraging clients to identify what is and is not already working to support them in their grieving process. When grieving clients build their strengths, they examine their own thought and behavior patterns and ask whether those patterns are helpful or unhelpful. They then work to reduce their unhelpful patterns and enhance the helpful patterns. As with the other categories of resilient grieving, building on strengths is not easy and takes real courage. Support your clients in building on strengths by gently guiding their reflections and helping them to define what "healthy" and "unhealthy" means to them.

BUILDING RESILIENCE ACROSS THE FOUR THEMES

Grieving clients can build resilience in many ways across each of the four themes of resilient grieving. Share with your clients the following themes and invite them to discuss their thoughts on each entry.

Cultivate Resilient Thinking

- Strive for a positive and hopeful outlook.

- Lean toward rational thinking and away from negative and catastrophic thoughts.

- Accept that change is part of life.

Lean into Supportive Relationships

- Prioritize and deepen your relationships.

- Join a grief group.

- Ask for support from friends, family, and community members.

Practice Emotion Management

- Prioritize physical health through healthy choices around food, exercise, and sleep.

- Practice mindfulness and meditation.

- Avoid unhealthy substances like alcohol and drugs.

Build on Strengths

- Identify the strengths that you've drawn on in past difficulties.

- Find ways to express those strengths now.

- Continue cultivating self-compassion.

EXPLORING PAST RESILIENCE

The *Exploring Past Resilience* worksheet is useful for supporting resilient grieving, in part because it fosters the identification of client strengths. The worksheet serves to provoke clients' reflections on times in the past when they have practiced resilience. Although their circumstances may have radically changed after their loss, they still possess the skill of resilience and can continue to cultivate it.

Introduce the worksheet in session when you feel a client understands the concept of resilient grieving. You may want to use the questions to guide an exploratory discussion to identify sources of resilience they may not have considered. Then, ask them to complete the worksheet outside of session, identifying a few more challenging times and reflecting on those experiences. Repeated practice will help show patterns of resilience that clients can consciously draw on as they continue to grieve.

EXPLORING PAST RESILIENCE

Begin by thinking about a time in your life that was demanding or difficult. Explain, in as much detail as possible, how you handled the situation and made it through to the other side.

What was a challenging time in your past?

_____

_____

_____

What was your goal?

_____

_____

_____

What challenges did you have to face?

_____

_____

_____

What kinds of difficult emotions did you experience?

_____

_____

_____

What personal skills helped you overcome the situation?

_____

_____

_____

What kind of mindset did you use to face the challenges?

_____

_____

_____

Did you accept support from the outside?

_____

_____

_____

How did you cope?

_____

_____

_____

On a scale of 1 to 10 (with 10 being the highest) what would you rate your resilience? _____

Based on this past experience, are there resilient techniques you can apply to your current situation?

_____

_____

_____

_____

_____

BUILDING SOCIAL SUPPORT

Accepting help from friends, family, and the community when clients are grieving can improve their well-being, self-esteem, physical health, and the ability to cope with stress. In most situations, social support is offered according to four different types:

1. **Emotional:** These are people who help us manage our emotions, show us empathy, and listen to us.

2. **Practical:** These are people who help us navigate things like finances, transportation, and childcare.

3. **Informational:** These are people who provide information, advice, and resources.

4. **Social:** These are people who provide love, nurturing, and connectedness.

As I've described in previous chapters, those who have survived the death of a loved one will experience isolation in almost all social situations at one point or another. Sometimes, grieving individuals choose isolation; sometimes, isolation is passively enforced by members of social groups who don't know how to interact with others after a death.

Moving through the grieving process will necessitate moving through isolation to the more connected period that characterizes the aftergrief. In fact, resilient grieving requires grieving individuals to continuously try to seek out and strengthen social support.

Help your clients break down the components of connection into more manageable chunks by using the *Building Social Support* worksheet. To prepare clients to complete the worksheet, share the three categories of activities that help to build social support and ask them to use this information to build their own network of assistance and encouragement.

Strengthen Relationships

- Stay connected to family and friends.
- Make important relationships a priority.
- Reach out to a wider circle of friends/acquaintances.

Increase Community Interaction

- Participate in clubs.
- Volunteer.
- Get involved in church or other institutions of faith.

Seek Professional Support

- Attend grief support groups.
- Find a therapist.
- Join an online grief community.

BUILDING SOCIAL SUPPORT

Use the following prompts to identify and build your social support network.

List three people, groups, or communities that provide you with social support:

1. _____

2. _____

3. _____

Describe how each of the above can help with your current emotional, practical, and social support needs.

1. _____

2. _____

3. _____

What are three steps you can take to better embrace your supports?

1. _____

2. _____

3. _____

What are some ways each of your supports could help with a specific challenge you are facing?

1. _____

2. _____

3. _____

FINDING PURPOSE

Resilient grieving assumes that life has purpose. When someone dies, it's easy and even natural for clients to feel like life is meaningless. They may feel as though their own life has lost its meaning in the aftermath of the death of their loved one. Or they might feel as though all of life is meaningless: If life can end at any time, and well before what seems like a more natural endpoint, they might feel that it's not just their own life that has lost its meaning. They may wonder if life itself is pointless and purposeless.

I don't have to tell you that this is a difficult and often deeply painful way to live. For some clients, it takes incredible resilience to retrain their focus from ruminating on their sense of life's meaningless.

You can support your clients as they grapple with finding meaning after their loss by working with them to cultivate self-compassion and find their purpose. Living with purpose enables engagement with life. It can give life meaning and result in deep satisfaction, even after a death of a loved one. Your grieving clients may feel a desire to disengage with life, but when they're ready, you can work with them to identify purpose in life after loss.

When clients open up to resilient grieving, begin a discussion with them to help them identify a purpose in life.

- Help clients identify ways they can help others.
- Help clients identify and move toward goals, both small and large.
- Help clients identify and seek out opportunities for self-discovery and growth.

I will discuss helping your clients find purpose, along with meaning and connection, in more detail in chapters 13 and 14.

CULTIVATING HOPE

Finding a purpose and cultivating hope go hand in hand. It is hard for clients to have hope if they don't have a purpose, and it is hard to find a purpose if they don't have hope. Note that I don't describe a purpose or hope as a feeling or a possession. This is important. It is common to assume that people simply "have" purpose or "have" hope. Some may feel this way and may experience their purpose and their hope in this way. However, many others do not, whether or not they have experienced the death of a loved one.

I believe that purpose and hope are action-oriented. All of us must *determine* our purpose. All of us must *foster* our hope. Like self-compassion and resilient grieving, purpose and hope are things we have to work to manifest. But when a client's loved one dies, the necessity of working toward these ends becomes much more obvious and much more difficult. Resiliently grieving means working to cultivate meaning, purpose, and hope, even when they feel hopeless.

Help your clients to cultivate hope by encouraging them to reflect on what hope means to them and by identifying their own sources of hope. This may be a difficult discussion for clients to engage in. Feeling hopeful after a death can cause many people to feel vulnerable and afraid. For this reason, it may be useful to explore this topic along with guided meditation.

 QUESTIONS FOR CLIENTS

Let's consider the concept of hope:

- What does hope mean to you?
- When have you used hope in your life?
- Have your hopes changed throughout your life?
- How has being hopeful or feeling hopeless influenced choices you've made?
- What gives you hope?
- What needs to happen for you to feel more hopeful in life?

MY SELF-COMPASSION AND RESILIENCE PLAN

My Self-Compassion and Resilience Plan offers a guide to the tools clients can use to cultivate self-compassion and resilience. The plan functions as a quick guide for clients, reminding them of the work they have already done to cultivate self-compassion and resilience, and supporting them in the steps they can take today to continue extending themselves compassion and facing their grief with courage.

 CLIENT PLAN FOR SELF-COMPASSION AND RESILIENCE

Let's reflect on the all the strategies for self-compassion and resilience you have experimented with over the course of our work together. Write a few ways you will cultivate resilience for each the following prompts:

- I will establish routines by . . .
- I will build connections by . . .
- I will make new friends by . . .
- I will take care of my physical health by . . .
- I will practice self-care by . . .
- I will manage my emotions by . . .
- I will feel gratitude by . . .
- I will volunteer or support others by . . .
- I will seek opportunities for self-discovery and growth by . . .
- I will cultivate hope by . . .
- I will pursue joy by . . .
- I will find purpose by . . .

REFLECTION

For some clients, cultivating self-compassion and resilience will be the most difficult work of their grieving process. It is not easy for them to feel self-compassion when they may feel they need to harden themselves to survive their grief. It is incredibly hard to choose resilience when they feel completely crushed by their loss. However, this is some of the most important work you will do when you serve as a companion to grief. If you use just a handful of resources from this workbook, I hope you use the resources on mindfulness and meditation and the resources on cultivating self-compassion and resilience. The tools associated with these practices can provide grieving clients with lifelong support.

CHAPTER 13

EXPLORING RELIGION, SPIRITUALITY, AND RITUAL

Rituals are the formulas by which harmony is restored.

—Terry Tempest Williams

As your clients move through the wider arc of grief, their focus will begin to turn from the work of encountering and processing their grieving expressions to the work of integrating their loss into their lives. Grieving people are sometimes surprised to experience this shift. They may have approached their grief as I did; back then, I thought my main goal was to move on as quickly as possible through my grieving process. I had to learn, sometimes through hard experience, that we don't move past our loss. Our loss becomes a part of who we are and all we do.

This shift in focus can be a wonderful gift, and it offers many opportunities to express self-compassion and cultivate resilience, but it's a bittersweet one. Most everyone would prefer an embodied connection with their loved one in the here and now. Death makes this impossible, requiring the new connection with their person to take an intangible, spiritual form. Clients can and will continue to mourn this radically unfair compromise. However, they can also strengthen and honor the bond with their person—one that transcends death.

During this period, therapists and mental health professionals serve as a companion to clients' grief by supporting their efforts to explore what it means to sustain and strengthen their connection to their loved one. This often means helping clients to navigate the passage of time, sometimes through religious, spiritual, or other ritualistic practices.

Studies show that people who profess stronger spiritual beliefs seem to be able to move through the grieving process with more ease after the death of a loved one compared to people with no spiritual beliefs. Religious and spiritual beliefs can also lend a larger sense of meaning to a loved one's life and death. For some, maintaining beliefs that their person remains in *some* form, either being taken care of in the hereafter, preparing for reincarnation, or perhaps looking after their loved ones on Earth, can offer peace, generate connection and even relieve some anxiety. This is worth fostering, and it can be done in religious, agnostic, or atheistic ways.

In this chapter, I offer activities for supporting clients as they explore the religious, spiritual, or ritualistic activities that can strengthen their relationship with their loved one who has died. Although the activities can be used during session, clients often benefit from completing the activities on their own in conjunction with experimentation and reflection.

Many of the activities in this chapter touch on finding new meaning and purpose as clients manage the passage of time from their loved one's death. In the next chapter, I will discuss ways you can support your clients as they continue to find meaning and purpose in the aftergrief.

PREPARING TO EXPLORE RELIGIOUS AND SPIRITUAL BELIEFS AND PRACTICES

Approaching religion, spirituality, and ritual with grieving clients requires many of the same skills I've introduced in earlier chapters. You must prepare yourself for open, nonjudgmental, active listening. You must strive to serve as a supportive companion to grief. It is also worth noting that in a client's exploration of religion, spirituality, and ritual, they (both collectively and individually) will express a very broad range of views.

Some of those views may contradict or potentially undermine your own understandings, and this might occasionally pose challenges. Religion, spirituality, and ritual can be very personal aspects of every individual's experiences. Not everyone is open to engaging in exploratory discussions about these aspects. Further, you have your own views that you may or may not be willing to share.

Despite the potential challenges, it is your job to remain curious and respectful about all aspects of your clients' grieving process. Religion, spirituality, and ritual may be personal subjects—for your clients and for you—but they touch so closely on the search for meaning and purpose that it is worth navigating any potential discomfort.

WHAT TO EXPECT: EXPLORING RELIGION AND SPIRITUALITY

Grieving individuals frequently examine their beliefs in the wake of loss. Death shakes up all prior understandings of life and the afterlife in such profound ways that almost all grieving people must work to find new meaning and purpose in life. This typically requires clients to deeply reflect on their prior beliefs and convictions, regardless of whether they identify as religious, spiritual, agnostic, atheistic, or something else.

Your clients' spiritual inquiries may take many forms. Clients may feel newly religious or newly irreligious. They may long to explore conventional expressions of spirituality or very unconventional expressions. They may engage in new rituals, or old rituals may take on new importance. On the other hand, some clients might discard old rituals, or they might struggle to find a ritual that resonates with them and that they find fulfilling.

As you accompany your clients on the religious and spiritual parts of their grieving journey, it is also incredibly useful to both mark the passage of time and to help clients see passing time as something meaningful.

COMMUNICATING RESPECT FOR RELIGION AND SPIRITUALITY

You can communicate your respect for clients' consideration of religion, spirituality, and ritual in part by recalling some of the tenets of active listening described in chapter 2. Your goal is to hold space for your clients' exploration, which you can do by displaying the following communication skills:

- **Listening:** Work on listening to *hear* rather than listening to *respond*. It is not your job to change a client's belief system or their ways of thinking.

- **Considering:** Explicitly invoke your own empathy by putting yourself in your clients' shoes. Their grieving experience may have led them to radically different conclusions about religion, spirituality, or ritual than you've reached or than those reached by other clients.

- **Asking:** Communicate an attitude of curiosity and inquisitiveness by asking insightful questions to help clients explore their own beliefs, doubts, and fears more fully.

- **Learning:** Recognize the benefit of dynamic interactions by understanding your work with clients as a continual prompt to actively explore your own attitudes, beliefs, and values about spirituality, religion, and ritual. Your engagement with these aspects of life is fluid and can change.

- **Knowing:** Express confidence in your knowledge and in your ability to recognize the limits of your understanding of clients' spiritual or religious perspectives. It is important to recognize your limitations as a cue to provide clients with resources for referral and further exploration.

ON GRIEF AND PSYCHIC MEDIUMS

In their search for meaning after their person's death, it is very common for grieving individuals to seek answers from psychic or other spiritual mediums. Psychic mediums have had a long-standing relationship with death and grief, as humanity has always appointed certain individuals to act as intermediaries between life and death. For many grieving clients, a psychic serves as today's intermediary.

For a long time, I was skeptical about the use of psychic mediums in grief work. Over the years, I have become much more open to the idea, if only because so many of my clients want to process their experiences in this way.

I now believe that if a visit with a psychic medium helps a client to feel better connected or more peaceful about the loss of their loved one, then that is a good thing. When clients inquire about mediums, I take a particular approach, which is described in the following list. While your own approach may differ, it will be useful to consider how you will handle the subject of psychics and other spiritual mediums, given that they will likely be a part of the grief journey of many clients. Here is my approach to a client who is interested in or has visited with a psychic medium:

- If a client asks me if I think they should see a psychic medium, I like to ask them what they are hoping to get out of the experience and how they will feel if they do not receive this.

Processing their expectations can help limit hurt and disappointment if the experience is not a positive one.

- If a client wants to tell me about a session they have had with a psychic medium, I do my best to remain open. I sometimes listen as though they are telling me about a dream, and I look for symbolism as a way of helping the client to interpret meaning and value.

- If a client has had a negative experience with a psychic medium, I review with them what they were hoping to achieve and strive to help them come up with alternative ways to achieve the sense of connection, alleviation of guilt, or longing for peace.

- While I do know of a handful of psychic mediums that I trust, I only ever give referrals to them if my client asks and if we have thoroughly reviewed their expectations for the experience.

QUESTIONS FOR THERAPISTS AND MENTAL HEALTH PROFESSIONALS

Many clinicians who work with grief are deeply engaged with their religious and spiritual views. Take a moment to consider your beliefs and how they may affect your work:

- How do your spiritual or religious beliefs affect your views of grief and death?
- Do you have any biases or triggers in this area that you need to be aware of?
- How can your spiritual or religious beliefs help or hinder your work?
- Do any of the previous communication skills pose a particular challenge? How will you handle this or other challenges associated with communicating openness to client inquiries?
- What do you think about psychic and other spiritual mediums? How will you approach this subject with interested clients?

ACTIVITIES FOR EXPLORING RELIGION AND SPIRITUALITY

As your clients express an interest or other indications of readiness to explore religion and spirituality, you can invite them into a broad conversation with the questions that follow. Clients may view some or all of these questions as big or complicated. They may also struggle to answer some of these questions, or they may explain that their grief has made them incapable of answering some of them. This is to be expected. Part of the utility of inviting clients into a broad discussion is that it sheds light on some of the challenges clients face as they consider religion and spirituality in their grieving process. If a client struggles to respond or feels that some of the questions are impossible to answer, remind them that questions about religion and spirituality are open-ended and more of an invitation to exploration than a requirement to express a belief.

You can help guide exploration by setting the tone for a dynamic conversation. For instance, I will often share with clients my own views on religion, spirituality, and the afterlife. I also occasionally share how these have changed and how they will likely continue to change over time. Sometimes, offering clients this view from what they may perceive to be "the other side" of the grieving process can help them feel more comfortable wrestling with these questions too.

(?) QUESTIONS FOR CLIENTS

Let's consider your views on religion or spirituality:

- Do you have any spiritual or religious beliefs?
- Do you believe in a god or a higher power? What is your concept of God?
- How do these beliefs affect your grief?
- What do you find comforting in your beliefs?
- Do any aspects of your beliefs cause you anger or anxiety?
- Do you feel pressure from your family with regard to religious or spiritual beliefs?
- Was your loved one spiritual or religious?
- If you are not spiritual or religious, would you like to be?
- What do you think happens when we die? What did your loved one believe?
- Do you feel that your beliefs dictate your grief process or your ability to feel connected to your loved one?
- Where do you find a sense of connectedness?
- Do you believe we have a soul?
- Do you engage in a practice that makes you feel close to a higher power?
- Do you find comfort in prayer?
- Have you ever had a spiritual or religious experience that was meaningful?
- Does your spirituality or religion give you a sense of purpose?
- Do you find spirituality or religion to be a source of strength or hope?
- Are there any religions or schools of spirituality that you are curious about?
- Are you open to exploring new beliefs or expanding your current beliefs?

IDENTIFYING RELIGIOUS AND SPIRITUAL BELIEFS

While a broad conversation can provide a comprehensive view into a client's belief system, it is also useful to gain a snapshot of their current approach to religion and spirituality. This helps therapists and mental health care professionals shape treatment to suit clients' needs. It can also help clients to clarify for themselves their current needs and wants in terms of religion and spirituality.

In previous chapters, clients were encouraged to generate a snapshot of their experiences by completing an inventory, but an inventory activity is not particularly suited to this chapter's topics. To gain deeper insight into clients' current positions in relationship to their beliefs, ask them to indicate the statements in the following worksheet that best describe their current experience of religion and spirituality. Then, use their answers to deepen an in-session discussion or guide clients in an identification of potential avenues for further exploration.

IDENTIFYING RELIGIOUS AND SPIRITUAL BELIEFS

Put a check mark by the following statements that apply to your current beliefs.

- ☐ I am embracing preexisting beliefs.
- ☐ I am revisiting preexisting beliefs.
- ☐ I am feeling numb or disconnected from preexisting beliefs.
- ☐ I am feeling angry with preexisting beliefs.
- ☐ I am rejecting preexisting beliefs.
- ☐ I am questioning the existence of higher power.
- ☐ I am searching for faith.
- ☐ I am exploring new beliefs.
- ☐ I am adopting new beliefs.

EXPLORING RELIGIOUS AND SPIRITUAL BELIEFS

Depending on where clients are in their grieving journey, what their views are, and what their current relationships are with religion and spirituality, I often suggest the following activities to clients to inspire their further exploration.

Open a discussion with clients about the options in the following worksheet. If they are able to point to specific areas of interest, work with them to brainstorm appropriate opportunities for each option. Then, encourage them to choose one or more options and create a plan for their participation. Once they've participated, follow up with a discussion about their experiences.

EXPLORING RELIGIOUS AND SPIRITUAL BELIEFS

Put a check mark by the following activities that sound like they might be interesting to try. Then, describe your plan for when and where you will engage with the activities.

☐ Attend a spiritual or religious service.

_____

_____

_____

☐ Read spiritual or religious books.

_____

_____

_____

☐ Speak with a spiritual or religious leader.

_____

_____

_____

☐ Listen to podcasts about spirituality and religion.

_____

_____

_____

☐ Write letters to a higher power.

_____

_____

_____

☐ Talk to a higher power.

_____

_____

_____

☐ Prayer and meditation.

_____

_____

_____

☐ Attend spiritual or religious retreats.

_____

_____

_____

☐ Join online communities.

_____

_____

_____

☐ Talk with other seekers.

_____

_____

_____

☐ Go to conferences and workshops.

_____

_____

_____

ACTIVITIES FOR EMBRACING RITUAL

Discussions about religion and spirituality in the grieving process dovetail with discussions about rituals. Grieving rituals can be instrumental to helping clients work through, as well as honor, their grief. They help grieving individuals mark the passing of time while also honoring their loved one. Rituals also create opportunities for clients to focus their attention on deeply connecting with their loved one.

However, because the use of ritual varies so much in between different religions, spiritual traditions, and cultures, your clients may or may not be open to or aware of all the different benefits and uses of rituals. Rituals can be small, everyday acts, such as lighting a candle and thinking about a loved one. They can also be larger ceremonies, like funerals and sitting shiva.

Rituals can be especially helpful to integrate into holidays or anniversaries. These dates are typically already marked by a variety of rituals, though we don't always recognize the acts we perform on these days as such. Creating new rituals allows clients to include their loved one in these special days, even when they can no longer participate in the same ways.

Although I feel rituals are a good topic to explore alongside spirituality and religion, it is important to note that the timeline for exploring these elements look different for everyone. For some, finding meaning and creating ways to honor their loved one is something that can only come later, after the hard work of learning to feel and process more immediate emotions and feelings associated with grief. For others, finding meaning and honoring their loved one is present from the very start of the grief journey. If your clients aren't ready to discuss rituals, that's okay. Conversely, if a client wants to discuss rituals when telling their story of loss, that makes sense too.

GRIEF RITUALS

Although rituals can help create meaning and fulfill a sense of purpose, it can be hard for clients to think about rituals that will feel both meaningful *and* natural to them. The question of how to integrate rituals into their daily lives can also pose a challenge. It can be useful to remind clients that rituals offer an opportunity to explore different kinds of meaning-making. They can experiment with different possibilities for creating and observing rituals until they find one that feels right.

To support clients' exploration, follow up a discussion of rituals with the *Grief Rituals* worksheet, asking clients to reflect on the questions and write down answers in advance of the next session. Then, use their answers to guide an in-session conversation.

GRIEF RITUALS

Reflect on the rituals of grief. Write down your responses with as much detail as possible and bring your answers to the next session.

What does ritual mean to you?

_____

_____

_____

_____

_____

What grief-related rituals have you participated in that have been meaningful?

_____

_____

_____

_____

_____

In what ways do you feel ritual can be helpful to your grief process?

_____

_____

_____

_____

_____

Are there rituals you know of that you would like to use?

_____

_____

_____

_____

_____

_____

If you were to create your own ritual what would it be?

_____

_____

_____

_____

_____

_____

THE FOUR TYPES OF RITUALS

According to Dr. Kenneth Doka, an author and grief expert, four types of rituals can be helpful in the grief process. To foster further thinking about ritual, introduce the four types of ritual to clients, and then guide them in brainstorming possible options for rituals they might create for each type. Ask clients to continue reflecting on rituals out of session, writing down their ideas for different rituals on *The Four Types of Rituals* worksheet.

- **Rituals of Continuity:** These are rituals that enhance the feeling of a continued bond with a loved one who has died. This might look like creating a ritual around visiting the gravesite every week or lighting a candle for them every day.

- **Rituals of Transition:** These are rituals that mark a change in the grief journey. This might look like developing a ritual around donating a loved one's belongings or removing a wedding ring.

- **Rituals of Affirmation:** These are rituals that help to process emotions associated with a loved one. This might look like writing a letter to them on a particular occasion or carrying on a tradition in their name.

- **Rituals of Intensification:** These are rituals that mark the passing of time, including the commemoration of anniversaries or holidays. This might look like developing a ritual around a particular tradition someone used to share with a loved one.

THE FOUR TYPES OF RITUALS

Review Dr. Kenneth Doka's four types of ritual. For each type, describe a ritual that would honor your loved one.

Rituals of Continuity: Rituals that enhance the feeling of your continued bond with your loved one.

_____

_____

_____

_____

Rituals of Transition: Rituals that mark a change in your grief journey.

_____

_____

_____

_____

Rituals of Affirmation: Rituals that help to process emotions associated with your loved one.

_____

_____

_____

_____

Rituals of Intensification: Rituals that commemorate your anniversaries and passages of time.

_____

_____

_____

_____

PERSONAL COMMITTAL RITUAL

Sometimes, when a loved one dies, clients aren't able to attend their funeral, memorial, or other service. At other times, a service like this simply doesn't happen. In these circumstances, work with your clients to determine whether creating a committal ritual might help provide a sense of closure.

Although committal rituals are designed to help people say goodbye to their loved one, they are not just an opportunity for closure. They also present an opportunity for your clients to feel connected to the person who has died and to express love, closeness, and admiration for them.

If clients are interested in creating a committal ritual, support them with the *Personal Committal Rituals* worksheet. Ask clients to fill it out on their own, then discuss their choices in session, perhaps helping them to plan the ritual at the same time.

PERSONAL COMMITTAL RITUAL

Design your own committal ritual by responding to each prompt with as much detail as possible.

Where and when would you like your committal ritual to occur?

_____

_____

_____

_____

_____

Will you have friends or loved ones present or will you do this individually?

_____

_____

_____

_____

_____

_____

Is there any music you would like to play?

_____

_____

_____

_____

_____

_____

Are there any photographs you would like to display?

_____

_____

_____

_____

_____

Is there anything you would like to say during this time?

_____

_____

_____

_____

_____

Are there any other objects would you like to include? (e.g., flowers, candles, other items of meaning)

_____

_____

_____

_____

_____

LIST OF GRIEF RITUALS

When clients have a difficult time thinking of a meaningful ritual, when they feel pressure to create a ritual, or when they want to continue exploring ritual but aren't sure how, share with them the *List of Grief Rituals* worksheet. There are many different ways to create meaningful rituals. In fact, almost any act can become a ritual if that's the intention. Encourage your clients to use this list for ideas to think about creating new rituals in their lives. Help them actuate their ideas by thinking through when rituals might bring them comfort and by planning when they might try out their new rituals.

LIST OF GRIEF RITUALS

Put a check mark by the following rituals that you might like to try. You can also use these ideas as the basis for creating your own ritual. These can be done sporadically, daily, or in conjunction with anniversaries and holidays.

- ☐ Light a candle and think of your loved one.
- ☐ Watch videos or go through photos of your loved one.
- ☐ Travel to a place that was meaningful to your loved one.
- ☐ Travel to a place your loved one always wanted to visit.
- ☐ Visit a burial or memorial site.
- ☐ Write a letter to your loved one.
- ☐ Write a story or poem about your loved one.
- ☐ Cook your loved one's favorite meal.
- ☐ Enjoy a meal at your loved one's favorite restaurant.
- ☐ Listen to your loved one's favorite music or songs.
- ☐ Watch your loved one's favorite movie or show.
- ☐ Release butterflies or balloons.
- ☐ Create art that relates to your loved one or your grief.
- ☐ Create a memory book of your loved one.
- ☐ Throw flowers into a body of water.
- ☐ Collect items that were meaningful to your loved one.
- ☐ Give yourself a gift from your loved one.
- ☐ Create an altar for your loved one.
- ☐ Carry a special item belonging to your loved one with you.
- ☐ Wear something belonging to your loved one.
- ☐ Host a family memory evening in which everyone brings a memory to share.
- ☐ Plant a tree or memorial garden.
- ☐ Donate to a cause that was important to your loved one.
- ☐ Volunteer for something in your loved one's honor.
- ☐ Create a scholarship in your loved one's name.
- ☐ Create a nonprofit in your loved one's name.
- ☐ Purchase a book in your loved one's name and donate it to a school or library.
- ☐ Share your loved one's favorite recipes with family and friends.
- ☐ Name someone after your loved one.

DESIGN YOUR OWN RITUAL

Asking clients to design their own ritual is a culminating activity: It is best introduced after completing the preceding activities, which helps clients to articulate their religious and spiritual beliefs and any relationship that may exist between those beliefs and rituals. Then, after you've worked with your clients to approach the different possibilities for using rituals to maintain a connection with their loved one, and after they've been able to experiment with a few rituals of their own, encourage them to design their own ritual.

It can be useful to use the questions on this worksheet as prompts to a preparatory discussion about creating new rituals. Once clients feel comfortable defining ritual and thinking through how they want to embrace ritual, they can then complete the worksheet on their own.

DESIGN YOUR OWN RITUAL

Answer the following questions with as much detail as possible to create a ritual to help you in your grieving process.

How do you define a ritual?

_____

_____

_____

_____

_____

How can you embrace ritual in your grieving process?

_____

_____

_____

_____

_____

Are there large rituals you would like to create to commemorate certain anniversaries or holidays?

_____

_____

_____

_____

_____

_____

Are there small rituals you can use daily?

_____

_____

_____

_____

_____

What elements are meaningful to you in a ritual? (e.g., music, candles, photos)

_____

_____

_____

_____

_____

Describe the ritual you would like to create and what it means to you.

_____

_____

_____

_____

_____

CREATING RITUALS AROUND HOLIDAYS AND ANNIVERSARIES

Holidays and anniversaries, which are unavoidable after a loss, are some of the most difficult days a grieving client will experience. This is not only because these important days mark the passing of time, but because they are often characterized by the rituals that they shared with their loved one who has died.

There are so many different kinds of anniversaries and holidays that people celebrate, and each one brings its own unique challenges. Help clients find ways to navigate these tough days by integrating new or different rituals to mark the passage of time. Taking this step before these dates occur can help alleviate clients' anxiety and help them feel prepared to face the days when they come. Holidays, anniversaries, and other related days that may be difficult can include:

- Birthdays (e.g., client, loved one, family members, friends)
- Anniversary of when your client met their loved one
- Wedding and other relationship anniversaries
- Anniversary of when your client's loved one became ill
- Anniversary of your client's loved one's death (this is also the anniversary of your client's grief process)
- Father's Day
- Mother's Day
- Valentine's Day
- Easter
- Passover
- Fourth of July
- Rosh Hashanah
- Halloween
- Thanksgiving
- Hanukkah
- Christmas
- New Year's Eve

The holidays and anniversaries will continue to arrive, but old traditions and rituals that once marked that day may feel lost to your clients. Often, it is only after they're able to express their emotions and feelings about these many losses that they can turn to the work of creating new rituals that will include and honor their loved one.

Use the following prompts to guide a discussion about your clients' fears and hopes around holidays and anniversaries.

(?) QUESTIONS FOR CLIENTS

Let's talk about holidays and anniversaries:

- What holidays or anniversaries do you connect with your loved one?
- How will it feel to experience these particular dates, anniversaries, and holidays in their absence?
- What are some ways you can emotionally prepare for these dates and occasions?
- How do you want to spend these dates and occasions?
- If you want to commemorate a holiday or anniversary, what rituals do you want to use?
- How can you honor your loved on these dates and occasions?
- Are there new rituals or traditions you want to create for particular anniversaries or holidays?
- If it is too painful to observe or honor your loved one on a particular date or anniversary, are there other ways you can spend the day, either distracting yourself or practicing self-care?
- What are some ways your family and friends can support you around these dates and occasions?

SOCIAL MEDIA-BASED RITUALS AND REMEMBRANCE

We cannot speak about establishing new rituals around loss without also discussing social media. Social media has made it easy for people to acknowledge their loved one's birthday and other important dates to their social networks. Some people integrate social media-based rituals around these dates by sharing photos and memories.

However, navigating social media following the loss of a loved one can be difficult. Some find it useful as an outlet to express their grief or honor their loved one, while others find it intrusive or too public a space to incorporate into their grieving process.

Because social media is a prevalent part of modern life, it is important to talk with clients about how they might utilize it in their grief process. It's important to explain to clients that this is an individual and evolving choice. It may feel good to post photos and memories of their loved one on anniversaries or holidays. But it might also feel bad, and they may want to stay off social media around these occasions. That's okay too.

It can be helpful to point out that social media is also a means by which clients can find and follow accounts about grief or those that are related to their particular loss. This can provide a sense of community and help them find advice, ways to cope, and ideas for making meaning after loss. Have an in-session discussion with your clients about what they are comfortable sharing, reminding them that they can change their minds at any time.

QUESTIONS FOR CLIENTS

Let's consider how you might want to approach social media in regard to your grief:

- Does social media feel good to you? Why?
- When does social media trigger you?
- What are some ways you can avoid being triggered?
- How do you want to handle social media during holidays and anniversaries?
- Are there ways you want to use social media to honor your loved one?

MY RELIGION, SPIRITUALITY, AND RITUALS PLAN

My Religion, Spirituality, and Rituals Plan offers a guide to the tools clients can use to explore the different aspects of religion, spirituality, and rituals that may help them express new meanings and purposes in life after their loved one has died. The plan functions as a quick guide for clients, reminding them of the many options they can pursue to continue their exploration.

 CLIENT PLAN FOR RELIGION, SPIRITUALITY AND RITUALS

Let's reflect on the work we've done together concerning religion, spirituality, and ritual. Write a few ways you will continue to explore these areas as you continue to travel along your grieving journey:

- I will explore religion by . . .
- I will explore spirituality by . . .
- I will explore rituals by . . .

REFLECTION

Older models of grief may have implied that grieving individuals must move on after their person's death. We now recognize that this is not possible. Your clients cannot and will not forget their loved one's place in their life, even if they might think that doing so could save them from the pain of grief. Religion, spirituality, and rituals offer a wide variety of ways to maintain connections with a loved one who has died. Religion and spirituality offer different avenues for exploring, approaching, and understanding the afterlife and the spirit world. Rituals do this too, but they also offer clients accessible ways to integrate and honor their loved one in their everyday experiences. Supporting your clients as they explore ways to establish and maintain their connection to their loved one can offer them purpose, meaning, and eventually, peace.

CHAPTER 14

FINDING CONNECTION AND PURPOSE

Goodbyes are only for those who love with their eyes. Because for
those who love with their heart and soul, there is no separation.

—Rumi

There is nothing easy about moving through the grieving process. The early path of grieving is strewn with intense emotional challenges. Further along the journey, the challenges may feel less emotionally immediate but can still be fraught with anxiety, anger, guilt, and every other emotion on the spectrum. It can be difficult to forge new connections in the wake of a major loss—especially the connections your clients have with their loved one.

However, every step along this path is worth it because it leads your clients closer to creating a new relationship with their loved one who has died. In all my work, I've found this—the work of sustaining and even strengthening a client's new relationship with their person—to be the most challenging yet most rewarding part of the grief journey.

Clients sometimes view the task of forging a spiritual or an internal relationship as nearly impossible. Unlike the established precedents you can draw on when exploring religion, spirituality, and rituals, there are no obvious examples for what a relationship with a deceased loved one looks like. Even so, people who are grieving yearn for this relationship. By guiding and supporting their efforts, you can forge a link where it once seemed unimaginable. Over time, this can grow and evolve into a fulfilling relationship that offers connectedness and congruence.

In this closing chapter, I describe a variety of activities that will help clients invite their loved one into their lives. These activities include identifying the meaning of connection, providing aids for connection, and recognizing some of the obstacles clients may come across. I also discuss various possibilities for helping clients communicate with their loved one, including through reflective conversations and writing prompts. I then turn to the related work of finding purpose.

I close this book with the concept of purpose because for grieving individuals, finding purpose is truly ongoing work. The activities I offer in the pursuit of purpose are consequently open-ended and reflective. They help clients to consider, again and again, not just where they've come from, but where they want to go.

ACTIVITIES TO HELP CLIENTS FIND CONNECTION

Connection not only means different things to different clients, but it means different things to different clients at different times. When I'm working with clients who are going through a recent loss, I try to encourage them to find ways to continue to feel connected to their loved one. For clients with older losses, you might look for ways they can reconnect and create a new internal or spiritual relationship with their loved one who has died.

Most clients benefit from an exploratory discussion about what connection means to them or what it could mean in the context of grief. Start an open conversation with clients about their ideas of connection. It can be useful to explore these questions in session to gain a sense of their approach to connection and to allow them to become more aware of their own approach. You can also allow clients to reflect further on some of their answers out of session.

 QUESTIONS FOR CLIENTS

Let's talk about connection with your loved one:

- What does it mean to you to stay connected to your loved one?
- What are some ways you currently feel connected?
- What are some ways you'd like to feel more connected?
- Do you feel you have any blocks or resistance to feeling connected?
- Are there things you feel you need to do or put in place in order to stay connected?
- What are some ways you can create a stronger sense of connection?

CONVERSATIONS WITH YOUR LOVED ONE

For many people, conversations offer an opportunity for connection. We connect with acquaintances while chatting about the weather; we connect with friends while discussing personal problems and victories; we connect with our loved ones while conversing about all kinds of topics, great and small.

When a client's loved one dies, it can impact their ability to find connection through conversations. They might feel uncomfortable chatting with acquaintances—who may or may not know about their loved one's death. Clients may even feel incapable of conversing with friends about their struggles or pain. They may feel that the death of their loved one has cut off conversation with them forever, making all other conversations feel like a poor substitute.

We can support these clients by introducing them to conceptual conversations. Conceptual conversations allow clients to open conversations with their loved one who has died. Although it may sound strange at first, most people are capable of imagining what their friends and loved ones would say to them in a given circumstance. Some people may even call a parent, parental figure, or best friend to mind, imagining their response in the midst of a particular struggle.

But just because a loved one is no longer physically here does not mean a client cannot envision their guidance or encouragement. For instance, after my mom died, I often opened a conceptual conversation with her, asking her for advice about work situations and relationships. It was easy for me to imagine what she might say to me in response to these scenarios, and the conversations allowed me to connect with my mom even though she had died.

As you work with clients, you may find that they already hold these conceptual conversations with their person who has died. However, they may feel anxious, ashamed, or embarrassed by these conversations, viewing them as evidence that they haven't been able to let go or move on from the death of their loved one. In these cases, relieve your clients of their burden by pointing out that conceptual conversations can be a healthy way to continue connecting with their loved one after death.

In fact, you can support clients in establishing and strengthening their connection to their loved one who has died through the following prompts. Some of these prompts are simple ones so that clients can easily recall the kind of day-to-day conversations they may have had with their loved one. Other prompts are bigger and may provoke bigger and more complicated emotions and feelings.

Additionally, while some clients find immediate comfort in this activity, other clients may find the connection almost too much to bear. Some clients may yearn for connection to their person but fear that establishing it might provoke too much pain. For these clients, open up the possibility of conceptual conversations slowly, and take breaks for self-soothing activities as necessary. Encourage all clients to experiment with this activity by asking the question in their mind, closing their eyes, and listening for their loved one's response.

IN-SESSION ACTIVITY

Use the following prompts to open up a conversation with your loved one:

- What comforting words would you say to me right now?
- What do you think about how much I miss you?
- Will I ever be okay again?
- What can I do to feel close to you?
- What do you think about my relationship with my partner?
- What do you think I should do about my job?
- How should I redecorate my kitchen?
- How can I be a better parent?
- Do you like the outfit I'm wearing?
- Should I go on this trip?
- Should I make dinner or order takeout?
- Is it okay for me to be happy again?
- What were your favorite moments with me?
- What should I do to take care of myself?
- _____

WRITING TO STAY CONNECTED

Writing is an ideal medium for connecting with a loved one who has died. First, writing is already considered an aid for reflection: Many people use it as a tool for better understanding their thoughts, behaviors, and actions. Second, because it works as a reflective medium—a means by which people might work something out—it is as common for someone to write to themselves as it is to others. Third, when people write to themselves, as in a journal, they don't expect a response. Even text messages and emails to others require a period of silence before a response. For all of these reasons, writing is an ideal medium for fostering a connection to a loved one.

Explore with grieving clients the place of writing in their own lives, asking them to consider if they'd like to use writing as a tool for connection with their person. This may mean clients experiment with new writing habits, such as keeping a daily or weekly journal in which they record their thoughts about their loved one. It may mean writing down memories that they want to always remember. Or it may mean approaching old writing habits in new ways, such as developing a letter-writing ritual as a way to honor and connect with a loved one.

The suggestions that follow offer a variety of ways for clients to approach writing as a tool for connection. Discuss with clients which of the approaches feel doable. Then, help them plan to integrate one or more of the approaches into their lives.

 JOURNAL PROMPTS

Use these writing prompts to feel connected with your loved one:

- Keep a daily journal telling your loved one about your life.
- Keep a book of memories of your loved one that you don't want to forget.
- Write letters to your loved one about big things that happen in your life.
- Write down questions you want to ask your loved one, and meditate on the answers.
- Write down memories of your loved to pass on to children or other family members.
- Write down comforting things your loved one said to you.
- Write a letter to yourself from your loved one.
- Write a letter to another family member from your loved one.
- Write down dreams about your loved one.
- Write down signs you receive from your loved one.
- Write cards to your loved one on holidays and anniversaries.

EVERYDAY WAYS TO STAY CONNECTED

Clients may fear that maintaining and strengthening their connection to their loved one, through writing for example, may require more than they are able to give. Sometimes, for instance, a client may fear that integrating moments of connection will stimulate further grief or may make their grief more difficult to contain.

However, staying connected and strengthening a connection to a loved one can be as easy as identifying a simple intention and then fulfilling it. For example, after my dad died, whenever I used something he taught me in life, like how to balance a checkbook or change a showerhead, I decided to take a moment to feel gratitude and love for him and to talk to him in my head or out loud. When clients try to foster this same simple connection, they often find that it helps them feel closer to their loved one and soothes some of their grief.

When speaking with clients about everyday connection, consider opening up a brainstorming session to help clients envision a variety of commonplace ways they can connect with their loved one. In this context, "everyday" and "commonplace" refer to easy things clients can do to include their loved one in their life. For example, they might consider cooking their person's favorite dish every Friday. That's how I stay close to my mom. She was a chef, and when I make her special dishes, or when I simply invite my memories of her into the kitchen with me, I feel a deep and satisfying connection. Of course, clients don't necessarily have to do something active. A client might simply decide to frame favorite photos of their person and hang them around their house.

IN-SESSION ACTIVITY

Help clients generate a list of ideas for connection that feel special but also doable. Then, talk with clients about how they will implement these ideas into their lives. You can use these examples to get started:

- Cook your loved one's favorite dishes.
- Ask family and friends to share favorite memories of your loved one.
- Say prayers or blessings in your loved one's honor.
- Set an extra place in your loved one's honor at family gatherings or celebrations.
- Donate to a charity in your loved one's honor.
- Continue to uphold traditions that were meaningful to your loved one.
- Keep photos of your loved one in your home.
- Light a candle in your loved one's honor.
- Play your loved one's favorite music.
- Visit restaurants or places your loved one enjoyed.
- Visit your loved one's gravesite.
- Plant a flower or tree in your loved one's honor.
- Travel to a place your loved one wanted to visit.
- Write your loved one letters.

- Go to church or spiritual centers.
- Wear an item of clothing or jewelry that belonged to your person.
- Watch home movies or look through photos.
- Write about or to your loved one.
- _____

ACTIVITIES FOR FINDING PURPOSE AND MEANING

The activities I've described in this and the previous chapter will help clients work toward finding meaning in their lives after their loved one has died. Finding meaning after loss can be a complicated subject. For some clients, the phrase "finding meaning" might trigger painful feelings: As with finding purpose, they may feel as though they're being asked to look at the bright side of their person's death, and this can feel disrespectful as well as impossible. For others, the work of finding meaning can feel like too big a challenge. They may feel that they're simply trying to survive their loss—they can't or don't want to look to what they perceive to be larger questions.

Even so, the search for meaning reflects a near universal desire: As humans, we all generally want, and perhaps even need, to feel that life has meaning. Indeed, our belief that life has meaning supports our engagement in life. If we feel life doesn't have meaning, our actions and efforts in life can seem pointless.

The meaning of life is evident for some. They may not be able to identify or articulate the meaning of life, but they feel comfortable in their knowledge that it exists. This is not always the case for grieving people. Their proximity to death and the loss of their loved one may have thrown all meaning into question. They may have questions about meaning that they didn't have in the past. While I tend to think that the "meaning of life" has always been open-ended and complicated, I also believe that grieving people understand this more intimately than most.

You must support your grieving clients to find and—perhaps more importantly—to *create* meaning because doing so is an instrumental part of the healing process. Like forging a new sense of connection to a lost loved one, finding meaning is something that may come later in the grief process, but it's something that can be incredibly healing.

Different people find meaning in different ways and at different times, so it's useful to explore this topic repeatedly at different stages and during different phases in order to help clients grapple with the outstanding question of meaning-making. I like to open the topic by asking my clients big questions about meaning, especially how they view meaning in their own life. These questions will be difficult to answer, and that's okay. In fact, finding and creating meaning and purpose may be an ongoing project for grieving clients, one they continually contribute to as they walk their grieving journey.

 QUESTIONS FOR CLIENTS

Let's consider meaning and purpose:

- Do you feel like you have a sense of meaning and purpose?
- What meaning, if any, do you attribute to your loved one's death?
- Do you feel open to searching for meaning?
- Do you have a sense of purpose connected to your loss?
- What would a sense of purpose look like?
- What does it mean to live a meaningful life?

REFLECTING ON FINDING MEANING

For many people, whether they are in a grieving period or not, meaning emerges upon reflection. Clients may not know what meaning to assign to experiences and events until they take the time to think more deeply about them.

The following worksheet offers a variety of prompts to encourage your clients to reflect on their experiences and to consider the meaning that they might be able to draw from those experiences. Introduce the worksheet in session to stimulate an initial discussion. Then, ask them to reflect on and answer the questions out of session.

REFLECTING ON FINDING MEANING

Ask yourself the following questions and answer each one as fully as possible. Take as many breaks as you need while you reflect on your experience.

What have you learned from your loss?

_____

_____

_____

_____

What was important to you before the loss?

_____

_____

_____

_____

What has become important to you since my loss?

_____

_____

_____

_____

What values of your person do you admire?

_____

_____

_____

_____

What is this person's legacy?

_____

_____

_____

_____

What positive traits and values of theirs can you embody in your own life?

_____

_____

_____

_____

How did your person shape your life?

_____

_____

_____

_____

How did your person make you a better person?

_____

_____

_____

_____

Is there anything constructive you can do or create in their honor?

_____

_____

_____

_____

What are some ways you can help others with the knowledge you have gained from your person's death?

_____

_____

_____

_____

What are some ways you can keep their memory alive?

_____

_____

_____

_____

What are some ways you can feel joy?

_____

_____

_____

_____

What does a meaningful life look like for you?

_____

_____

_____

_____

Common Ways to Find Purpose and Meaning after Loss

There are many ways you can support your clients as they work toward finding meaning and purpose after a loved one's death. Help your clients think about how they may be able to create meaning and purpose after the death of their loved one. Once they are comfortable and have perhaps identified an option or two with which they want to move forward, help them begin to plan how to implement their ideas. Suggest to your clients these common ways to find meaning and purpose:

- Create a change in your life to honor your loved one.
- Create a foundation, movement, or project in your loved one's honor.
- Create an organization or take up a cause that works to prevent what happened to your loved one.
- Donate your loved one's organs.
- Explore the afterlife.
- Invest in spirituality or religion.
- Volunteer for hospice, cancer centers, or suicide hotlines.

Finding Meaning after Loss Aphorisms

Regardless of clients' views on finding meaning after loss, most can benefit from integrating aphorisms into their self-talk. Aphorisms offer pithy reminders of truth, and with the following examples, clients can self-soothe when their search for meaning and purpose starts to feel overwhelming. They can also use the aphorisms to shine a light when they feel they've reached a dead end.

I often introduce these aphorisms to clients and then offer them as a take-home resource. I then frequently integrate the aphorisms into our in-session discussions, modeling for clients the ways the statements can be used. Some examples can include:

- Finding meaning is an individual process.
- Finding meaning takes time.
- Finding meaning does not mean letting go or moving on.
- Finding meaning does not mean it's okay that your loved one died.
- Finding meaning can help me move forward.

REFLECTION

For those of us who have lost a loved one, finding meaning and purpose after their death is an active and ongoing pursuit. We must *make* meaning and *build* purpose. It is not easy, but we do this to honor our loved one and the full, meaningful, purposeful life they want us to live.

We also do this for ourselves. We will not—and we cannot—*make sense* of death. We can, however, learn to live with death and to grow beyond the physical limitations it seems to enforce. For instance, we can learn to view death not as an inevitable end to everything but as the beginning of a new relationship with our loved one. Indeed, after our person's death, we can strengthen our connection with our person and find our purpose in this connection, even though we no longer share a physical bond. We can do this. It is not easy. It is the opposite of easy. It is also the opposite of the life with our loved one that we may have envisioned. But with the support of a thoughtful, compassionate grief companion, we can emerge into the aftergrief with peace and even joy. We can make our loss meaningful, even as we mourn.

ABOUT THE AUTHOR

 **Claire Bidwell Smith, LCPC,** is a therapist specializing in grief and the author of multiple books, including *Conscious Grieving* and *Anxiety: The Missing Stage of Grief.* Led by her own experiences with grief and fueled by her work in hospice and private practice, Claire strives to provide support for all kinds of people experiencing all kinds of loss. Claire offers numerous programs in addition to working with people one-on-one, as well as training other clinicians to work in the field of grief and loss. Claire has been featured in and written for *The New York Times, The Atlantic, The Washington Post, Scientific American, The LA Times, CNN, MSNBC, Forbes, The Today Show, Goop, Oprah Magazine,* and *Psychology Today.* She deeply loves her work and is devoted to expanding the conversation about grief and loss. Find out more and connect with Claire at www.clairebidwellsmith.com.

For your convenience, purchasers can download and print the worksheets from this book at **www.pesipubs.com/anxiousgrief**